D0914958

WHAT I LEARNED ON THE WAY TO THE TOP

by
ZIG ZIGLAR

Honor Books
Tulsa, Oklahoma

2nd Printing

What I Learned on the Way to the Top
ISBN 1-56292-542-3
Copyright © 1998 by Zig Ziglar
3330 Earhart, Suite 204
Carrollton, Texas 75006-5026

Published by Honor Books, Inc.
Box 55388
Tulsa, Oklahoma 74155

The Bottom Line of Success

*In everything you do, put God first, and he will
direct you and crown your efforts with success.*

Proverbs 3:6 *TLB*

The bottom line of success is this: pleasing God. True success,
the kind of success that pleases God, can be measured in eight
crucial areas of life: happiness, health, finances, emotional
security, the quality of your friendships, family relationships, your
sense of hope, and an overall peace of mind.

I have filled this book with stories and challenges that will
encourage and inspire you to excel in the areas of your life that
matter most.

These meditations are designed to be easy to read. They would
make a great addition to your morning devotional reading, your
lunch break, or your wind-down time at the end of the day. They
only take a few minutes to read, but the truth you glean can have
an impact on you for life.

In addition to my own writing, I've included quotes from some
of the great people who have motivated me. I trust you'll be
inspired in the same way.

Be encouraged! Be challenged! Be blessed! Be successful! Keep
moving toward the top!

—Zig Ziglar

When we do
more than we are
paid to do, eventually
we will be paid more
for what we do.

Work hard and cheerfully at all you do, just as though you were working for the Lord and not merely for your masters.

Colossians 3:23 TLB

4

As a youngster working in a grocery store, I knew the young boy who worked in the store across the street. In those depression years, most stores, of financial necessity, carried a very limited inventory. Of course, this frequently led to shortages, and in these cases the merchants simply borrowed from one another.

Charlie Scott was the "runner" for the store across the street. I recall countless instances when Charlie would hit our front door at a dead run and sing out to the owner of our store, "Mr. Anderson, I need to borrow six cans of tomatoes!" Mr. Anderson always replied, "Well, go get 'em, Charlie. You know where they are." Charlie would dash back to the shelf, grab the items he was borrowing, quickly deposit them on the counter, scribble his name on the slip showing what he had gotten, and race off.

One day, I asked Mr. Anderson why Charlie Scott always ran everywhere he went. He replied that Charlie Scott was working for a raise, and he was going to get one. I then asked him how he knew Charlie was going to get a raise, and Mr. Anderson replied that if the man he was working for didn't give him one, he would!

Maintaining
the right attitude
is easier than
regaining the
right attitude.

Never be lacking in zeal, but keep your spiritual fervor, serving the Lord. Be joyful in hope, patient in affliction, faithful in prayer.

Romans 12:11-12

Let's look at five life attitudes. First is self-esteem. That's the way you feel about yourself. That feeling of your own worth influences every facet of your life.

The second attitude is love, which is your attitude towards others. Love—real love—always thinks in terms of what is best for the other person.

The third attitude is faith. Faith is your attitude towards God. It will influence your attitudes toward your fellow man and members of your family.

The fourth attitude is hope, which is your attitude towards your future. Alfred Adler, the psychiatrist, said, "Hope is the foundational quality of all change, and it is the great activator. It gets people moving towards an objective. Hope is the realistic expectation that something good is going to happen."

The fifth attitude is forgiveness, which deals with your past. Your ability to forgive others for any wrong-doing will have a tremendous bearing on your future. The person who damaged your past is negatively impacting your present, and will negatively influence your future unless you forgive him or her. Forgiveness is the wisest choice.

Maintain these five attitudes in your life, and you will be well on your way to the top!

When you
turn to God,
you discover
He has been facing
you all the time.

For the eyes of the LORD
are on the righteous,
and His ears are open
to their prayers.

1 Peter 3:12 NKJV

A recent survey revealed that 96% of Americans believe in God, 90% say they pray, and 41% say they attend religious services at least once a week or almost every week. These figures are nearly identical to a survey conducted in 1947, with the only exception being that the percentage of those who believe in God has gone up one percent.

Translation: 105 million Americans are in worship services every week. That's more than attend all of the major league baseball games, plus all NFL football games, all NBA basketball games—all year long. Need I remind you that virtually every paper devotes an entire section to what's going on in the world of athletics? By contrast, last year there were only 287 stories of significance in the national media about what was going on in the lives of people of faith.

Please don't misunderstand. I am an avid sports fan, but how many spectators have had their lives changed because they were at a game—versus how many people's lives were changed at a religious service?

I wonder what would happen if every person who goes to religious services each week were to write the editor of their newspaper a letter, suggesting they give more coverage to our faith.

Men of genius are
admired. Men of
wealth are envied.
Men of power are
feared, but only
men of character
are trusted.

—Arthur Friedman

Moreover thou shalt provide out of all the people able men, such as fear God, men of truth, hating covetousness ... to be rulers.

Exodus 18:21 KJV

Several years ago I was speaking at a trade school, with several hundred students in attendance. Early on, approximately one-third of the students were attentively listening. The other two-thirds were either reading or pretending to be asleep.

The local television station had gotten word that I was to be speaking at the school and sent a camera crew to get some shots. They walked in down the left-hand aisle, came up on stage, got behind me, and started filming the entire student body as they listened to the presentation.

An interesting phenomenon took place. One hundred percent of the students suddenly became alert, sat up straight, and became enormously attentive. The spotlight was on them.

In many ways the spotlight is always on all of us, as far as our morals, ethics, and responsibilities are concerned. Let's not get caught unaware. By conducting our lives as if the camera is on and the mike is open, we will be living with integrity. The picture we have of ourselves will be character based and non-hypocritical. We won't have to apologize for or explain tomorrow what we did today.

Make failure your teacher, not your undertaker.

Don't you know that this good man, though you trip him up seven times, will each time rise again?

Proverbs 24:16 TLB

Sometimes little irritations, mistakes, and failures come our way that are not earth-shattering or life-changing, but they cause a momentary stop in our progress. Sometimes we permit the little incidents to linger entirely too long and give us problems far beyond their significance. Let's say that you are caught in one of these situations, and at the moment you're not depressed, but you're not exactly on cloud nine either. As a result, you know that you are not as friendly or as productive as you would like to be, so you want to snap out of it. What do you do?

Step number one: acknowledge that you're in a funky mood; you've got the "blahs."

Step number two: recognize that your momentary switch from positive thinking to "stinkin' thinkin'" is neither permanent nor even life-threatening, so it won't be fatal. It's eventually going to end, so instead of waiting for a change in circumstances to bring an end to the "blahs," make a conscious decision to end them yourself! Which means you have once again accepted responsibility for improving your circumstances. When you take that responsibility, your circumstances will change and you will have turned a small tragedy into a big triumph.

Where you start is not as important as where you finish.

In all things God works for the good of those who love him, who have been called according to his purpose.

Romans 8:28

Just in case you have even a trace of PLOM ("poor little old me") disease and are saying, "But, Zig, you don't understand about my past," I've got a better idea for you. Instead of explaining why it won't work for you, let me tell you how it has worked for others.

A study of three hundred world-class leaders, including Franklin D. Roosevelt, Sir Winston Churchill, Clara Barton, Helen Keller, Mahatma Gandhi, Mother Teresa, Dr. Albert Schweitzer, and Martin Luther King, Jr., revealed that 25 percent of them had serious physical disabilities and an additional 50 percent had been abused as children or were raised in poverty.

The world-class leaders responded (positive) instead of reacted (negative) to what happened to them. Remember, it's not what happens to you; it's how you handle what happens to you that's going to make the difference in your life.

Neil Rudenstein's father was a prison guard and his mother a part-time waitress. Today, Dr. Neil Rudenstein is president of Harvard University. He says he learned very early in life that there is a direct correlation between performance and reward. Rudenstein and the three hundred world-class leaders personally learned that it's not where you start—it's where you finish—that counts.

These ten little two-letter words—*If it is to be, it is up to me*—are absolutely valid. The solution is to do it now.

For the gifts and calling of God are without repentance.

Romans 11:29 KJV

One reason people do not develop and use their talents is denial. Many people find it comfortable to deny a talent. After all, if they deny their talents, then perhaps they can persuade others that they really don't have anything to offer.

A second reason people don't use their talents is procrastination. They're going to use them in the nonexistent future on Someday Isle ("someday I'll"), which is a nonexistent island. Tomorrow is the greatest labor-saving device ever brought to light.

I believe fear (which is faith in reverse) is a third reason for not using our talents. Many people don't understand that failure is an event and not a person, so they decide to "play it safe" and not do anything at all.

The fourth reason people do not use their talents is irresponsibility. They find it more comfortable to blame other things and other people for their failures.

Some of the saddest words you'll ever hear are "what might have been." Speaker Vicki Hitzges puts it in a unique and different way when she asks, "Will you look back on life and say, 'I wish I had' or 'I'm glad I did'?" You do have a choice.

Love is not the basis for marriage; marriage is the basis for love. Being loved is the second-best thing in the world; loving someone is the best.

Love . . . does not hold grudges and will hardly even notice when others do it wrong.

1 Corinthians 13:4-5 TLB

The True Love Daily Checklist

1. Did I speak words of love to my mate today?
2. Did I act with love toward my mate today?
3. Was I patient with my mate today?
4. Was I kind to my mate today?
5. Was I jealous or envious of my mate today?
6. Was I proud or boastful to my mate today?
7. Was I selfish with or rude to my mate today?
8. Did I demand my own way with my mate today?
9. Was I irritable or "touchy" with my mate today?
10. Did I hold on to grudges against my mate today?
11. Was I glad when truth triumphed with my mate today?
12. Was I loyal to my mate today?
13. Did I believe in and expect the best from my mate today?
14. Did I use my strengths for my mate today?
15. Did I keep the faith with my mate today?
16. Did I find hope with my mate today?
17. Did I love my mate today?
18. Do I understand that the greatest strength is love?

The profile of
a wealthy person
is this: hard work,
perseverance,
and most of all,
self-discipline.

*Do you know a hard-working
man? He shall be successful
and stand before kings!*

Proverbs 22:29 TLB

The Louis Harris poll of people who earned more than $142,000 a year and had a net worth of over a half million dollars, not including their homes, described these successful people as being unexciting, middle-aged, and cautious. They emphasized family values and the work ethic. Eight-three percent of them were married. Ninety-six percent of them acquired their net worth through hard work, which means they denied themselves immediate gratification so they could have what they really wanted later. Eighty percent were politically conservative or middle-of-the-road, and they were relatively nonmaterialistic.

In other words, their goals went beyond money. Eight-five percent said that their major objective was to provide for their family (that's an attitude of responsibility). Only 11 percent rated owning an expensive car as being very high on their want list. The badges of success didn't matter to them nearly so much as family, education, and their business or job—not much excitement but lots of happiness. They had a good standard of living but, infinitely more important, they had an excellent quality of life. Persistence, consistency, discipline, and hard work (all of which are learned skills) made the difference. Their lives seemed to be in balance.

Remember—the "free" cheese is in a mousetrap.

For even when we were with you, we gave you this rule: "If a man will not work, he shall not eat."

2 Thessalonians 3:10

Years ago Paul Harvey described how Eskimos in the frozen North kill wolves. They take a razor-sharp knife, dip it in blood and freeze it. Next, they bury the handle of the knife in the frozen tundra with the blade sticking up. Wolves, attracted to the scent of blood, come to lick the blade. The cold numbs the wolf's tongue and by the time he reaches the blade he's unaware he is licking a sharp edge. As he begins to bleed, he licks even faster until ultimately he bleeds to death.

In many ways Paul Harvey was describing the way young people are lured into drug and alcohol traps. Early on, some drugs and alcohol make a person feel good and they enjoy the feeling. After a few "trips" on those drugs and alcohol, however, they begin to lose their sense of perspective and the drugs have less and less effect. This leads them to indulge in stronger, more potent drugs—and he or she is "hooked."

Interestingly enough, the wolf and the drug addict have another thing in common. Each wanted the same thing—namely, to give little or nothing and get a lot. A more successful formula is to give a lot, and you'll get a lot in return.

Inject people
with hope.

*I pray that God will help you
overflow with hope in him
through the Holy Spirit's
power within you.*

Romans 15:13 TLB

On Saturday, May 3, 1997, I had the privilege of attending a Special Olympics event with my family. Our granddaughter, Elizabeth, participated in two races and won a silver and a gold medal. She was excited.

The opening ceremonies, complete with color guard, speeches, master of ceremonies, salute to the flag, "Star Spangled Banner," and performances by a drill team were all spectacular to watch. However, the most moving sight was watching the opening parade. Many emotions were displayed, but the main one was the sheer delight of so many of the athletes—their smiles, the jumping up and down, the way they hugged each other, and the enthusiasm they displayed.

The master of ceremonies reminded us that just thirty years ago the "experts" believed that no mentally retarded person would ever be able to swim the length of an Olympic-size swimming pool or run a mile. But then he rightly observed that they did not measure the heart or the soul of these athletes.

Question: "What would happen if all of us used the same percentage of our ability that these special athletes use of theirs?" Seeing the athletes' commitment gave hope to those present that day. Remember, those who give hope to others are generally filled with hope themselves.

If a child lives with praise, he learns to appreciate.

—Dorothy Nolte

Lo, children are an heritage
of the LORD: and the fruit of
the womb is his reward.

Psalm 127:3 KJV

Children Live What They Learn

If a child lives with criticism,
He learns to condemn.
If a child lives with hostility,
He learns violence.
If a child lives with ridicule,
He learns to be shy.
If a child lives with shame,
He learns to feel guilty.
If a child lives with encouragement,
He learns confidence.
If a child lives with praise,
He learns to appreciate.
If a child lives with fairness,
He learns justice.
If a child lives with security,
He learns faith.
If a child lives with approval,
He learns to like himself.
If a child lives with acceptance and friendship,
He learns to love the world.

—Dorothy Law Nolte

The ladder of
success works like
any other ladder.
Very few have climbed
it with their hands
in their pockets.

*Hard work means
prosperity; only a fool
idles away his time.*

Proverbs 12:11 TLB

The finals of the U.S. Amateur Golf Championship of 1997 was one of the most exciting and dramatic golf events of the year. Playing in the finals were Steve Scott and Tiger Woods. On the eighteenth green, the final hole, Steve was one up, putting first. Tiger's ball was in Steve's putting line, so Tiger spotted his ball a club-head length away and marked it. Steve Scott putted and missed.

Tiger carefully circled the green, viewed every possible angle and was lined up to putt when Steve reminded him that he had not spotted his ball back in the original spot. Making the correction, Tiger sank the putt, and the match was thrown into "sudden death," which was won by Tiger Woods.

Here's the reason Steve Scott is such a marvelous role model. Had he not reminded Tiger that he had not respotted his ball correctly, and Tiger had stroked the putt, he would have been penalized two strokes and lost the championship.

That's what makes long-term winners. That was sportsmanship and integrity personified. Even though Steve lost the championship, he won something infinitely more important—self-respect and the admiration of literally millions of golfers all over the world. That's a role model in action.

It is not what
happens to you that
determines how
far you go in life;
it is what you
do with what
happens to you.

But despite all this,
overwhelming victory is ours
through Christ who loved us
enough to die for us.

Romans 8:37 TLB

One of the most remarkable men I've ever known is Charlie Wedemeyer. Charlie coached the Los Gatos high-school football team to the only state championship they've ever won. I remember the day I attended a practice session with Charlie and his team. He and I were carrying on an extended conversation from the sidelines when periodically an assistant coach would run up and ask questions. Without hesitation, Charlie, who had been watching intently during our entire conversation, would spell out the specifics he should follow.

The amazing thing is that the only parts of his body he can move are his eyes and mouth. Charlie Wedemeyer suffers from Lou Gehrig's disease. His wife, Lucy, is his interpreter. She reads his lips and effectively delivers the message.

Charlie has the most remarkable attitude and the greatest sense of humor I believe I have ever seen. Though travel arrangements are difficult, he regularly speaks to people in schools, businesses, prisons, and churches. He has something to say, and Lucy verbalizes it to the audience. He might be the only speaker in America who can't speak. Needless to say, his life and wife communicate a powerful message of hope, love, and a "never-give-up" spirit. They both have a passion to make a difference.

You will make a lousy anybody else, but you are the best "you" in existence. You are the only one who can use your ability. It is an awesome responsibility.

I praise you because I am fearfully and wonderfully made; your works are wonderful, I know that full well.

Psalm 139:14

Around the turn of the century near the town of Beaumont, Texas, a landowner was forced to sell portions of his land to feed his family. Then an oil company told him there could be oil on his property and offered to pay him royalties if he would permit them to drill. The landowner agreed, because he had nothing to lose.

When the well came in, it destroyed the wooden derrick, creating enormous excitement. Before they could cap the well, several hundred thousand barrels of oil had pumped out. That was the discovery of "Spindletop," the most productive single oil well in history.

The landowner became an instant multimillionaire— or did he? The answer is really "no." You see, he'd been a multimillionaire ever since he had owned the property. Unfortunately, he had no knowledge of that fact and consequently did not capitalize on it.

It is my personal conviction that inside all of us, there is incredible ability and talent, much of which is never recognized and used. My suggestion is simple: Get acquainted with yourself. Recognize, develop, and use what you've got. Who knows—maybe there is a "Spindletop" underneath. You've certainly got nothing to lose by doing a little drilling and exploring. Who knows what might come to the surface?

The parent who truly has a good self-image understands that real love demands they do what is best for the child.

Being punished isn't enjoyable while it is happening—it hurts! But afterwards we can see the result, a quiet growth in grace and character.

Hebrews 12:11 TLB

This morning I heard a fascinating conversation between a father and a talk-show host. The father said his two little boys had been put on probation, because they had been late to school nine times in the last sixty days.

A family council was called and they all (including Dad) accepted full responsibility for their parts in the scenario. The parents explained that each morning at exactly 7:30 they would leave the house for school. If the kids were not ready they would gather everything they were going to wear and head for the car. When they arrived at the school they would exit the car and walk into the school, whether they had their shoes on or not.

The parents accepted their responsibility for getting the kids up early enough to give them time to get dressed and have breakfast.

Getting to school on time teaches the entire family to accept responsibility, but especially those two little guys. If they had been allowed to "get by" with being late and showing irresponsible behavior, a negative pattern might have been established. The teacher who reported them, the parents who accepted responsibility, and the two boys are all going to be winners. That's a winning approach to life.

For a child,
love is spelled
T-I-M-E.

Think constantly about these commandments ... teach them to your children and talk about them when you are at home or out for a walk; at bedtime and the first thing in the morning.

Deuteronomy 6:6-7 TLB

A young man was to be sentenced to penitentiary. The judge had known him from childhood and was well acquainted with his father, a famous legal scholar. "Do you remember your father?" asked the magistrate. "I remember him well, your honor."

Then, trying to probe the offender's conscience, the judge said, "As you are about to be sentenced and as you think of your wonderful dad, what do you remember most clearly about him?"

"I remember when I went to him for advice, he looked at me from the book he was writing and said, 'Run along, boy; I'm busy!' When I went to him for companionship, he turned me away, saying, 'Run along, son; this book must be finished!' Your honor, you remember him as a great lawyer. I remember him as a lost friend." The magistrate muttered to himself, "Alas! Finished the book, but lost the boy!"

The workaholic approach to life seems to be growing in popularity. Strange as it may sound, the workaholic is lazy. It requires considerably more effort and risk to learn how to communicate effectively with your spouse. And it requires considerably more energy for the workaholic to learn to play with, deal with, and communicate with a child on his emotional level.

I've got to say "no" to the good so I can say "yes" to the best.

For physical training is of some value, but godliness has value for all things, holding promise for both the present life and the life to come.

I Timothy 4:8

I love to eat in cafeterias, and I especially like ones that are arranged so that I can view what's being offered before I get to the serving line. Several years ago the Redhead (my wife) and I went into a new cafeteria, and I had the opportunity to carefully evaluate what was being offered. This enabled me to quickly move down the line, telling the people behind the counter to give me some of this and this and this. That's very important, because regardless of how hungry you are, you cannot eat some of everything on the line.

I wanted to choose foods that I felt would not only taste good but would also be good for me. In short, I had to pass up a lot of good food to get the best.

That's the parallel between the cafeteria line of life and the cafeteria line for food. In life, we simply cannot be, do, and have everything in this big, beautiful world of ours. We need to choose, and the choices we make will ultimately determine how successful we are in the eight crucial areas of life: happiness, health, peace, prosperity, security, friendships, family, and hope. It's up to you to choose the best and pass up the good.

We deplete nature's natural resources by using them up. We deplete man's natural resources by failing to use them.

The man who had received the one talent went off, dug a hole in the ground and hid his master's money.

Matthew 25:18

Little Johnny was a "pistol." One Friday afternoon his teacher said to the class, "Students, if any of you have an unusual event take place this week-end, please remember it and tell us about it on Monday morning."

On Monday morning, Little Johnny sat at his desk, quivering with excitement. The teacher said, "Johnny, it looks like something exciting happened for you over the weekend."

With enthusiasm, Johnny said, "Me and my daddy went fishin' and caught seventy-five catfish, and they all weighed seventy-five pounds." The teacher said, "Now, Johnny, you know that simply did not happen." Johnny replied, "Yes, Ma'am, it did!"

"Now, Johnny, if I were to tell you that on the way to school this morning all of a sudden a big, grizzly bear appeared in front of me and was about to grab me when suddenly a little yellow dog appeared out of nowhere, jumped up, grabbed the grizzly bear by the nose, broke his neck and killed him dead, now Johnny, would you believe that?"

Johnny cheerfully replied, "Yes, Ma'am, I sure would! As a matter of fact, that's my dog!"

Our imagination brings creative solutions to many problems, so let's encourage our kids to use their creative imaginations in life.

It seems universally true that people who have direction in their lives go farther and faster and get more done in all areas of their lives.

Where there is no vision, the people perish: but he that keepeth the law, happy is he.

Proverbs 29:18 KJV

Andrew Gardner, an assistant vice president with Merrill Lynch, says they have as clients a large number of men and women from all walks of life who earn $100,000 a year. They are different in many ways. The only common ground they have is the fact that at any given time of the year, when asked where they are on their objectives, any of these $100,000-a-year income earners can tell you precisely what their accomplishments are up to that date.

It is a fact of life that you need to know where you are, as well as how to get where you want to be. David G. Jensen, from the UCLA School of Medicine, surveyed the people who attend public seminars I conduct. He divided them into two groups: Those who set goals and developed a plan of action to reach them, and those who took no specific action to set their goals.

The goal-setters earned an average of twice as much per month as the non-action group. Not surprisingly, the action group tended to be more enthusiastic, more satisfied with life and work, happier in marriage, and their overall health was better. It helps to know where you're going.

When you break goals into increments and start controlling your time, things begin to happen.

Teach us to number our days aright, that we may gain a heart of wisdom.

Psalm 90:12

44

Perhaps the greatest advantage of having a goals' program is the freedom that goes with having direction. When your goals are clearly defined and intelligently set, you have, in essence, taken a major step toward programming your left brain. That frees your right brain to be its creative best.

The best analogy I can give you is the superbly conditioned and gifted athlete who is so disciplined and committed to the fundamentals of the game that he or she is free to be at their creative best.

Michael Jordan, for example, is confronted a number of times in every game he plays with a new situation. Because Michael is so drilled in the fundamentals, he, with his superb athletic skills, can be creative in the way he handles the truly unique situations that arise.

The same situation happens to all of us. Only with discipline, do doctors, students, and people like you and me have the freedom to give their best performance. When we are fundamentally sound with a base of moral, ethical values to work from, a goals' program to focus on, and the optimistic outlook of automatically seeking the solutions to problems with the expectancy of finding those solutions, we free the creative right brain to do exactly that.

By the mile it's a trial, but by the inch it's a cinch.

For precept must be upon precept . . . line upon line; here a little, and there a little.

Isaiah 28:10 KJV

James Bostick was six years old, had an intense dislike for school, did not like his teacher, and was making poor grades. He cried at night, complained of nightmares, and parent-teacher conferences were regular events for his mother, Laura.

In the course of events, James' parents divorced, and Laura took a class on developing the qualities of success. She realized that the missing ingredients in James' learning process were the qualities of honesty, enthusiasm, positive thinking, and respect—the qualities that, in general, make an individual more pleasant and successful. Laura started teaching the meaning of these skills to her son. She also cut out small "I CAN" circles and used them to reward James for improvement. She challenged him to do better in school and required him to tell her something good he had discovered about his friends and teacher every day.

It happened slowly, but during the year James changed. His grades showed drastic improvement and moved him to the top portion of his class. He won the first-place blue ribbon in the science fair competition for his class. His mother's efforts were rewarded when the young boy who begged to stay home was singled out for his achievements and honored with the "Student of the Week" award.

Some people find fault like there was a reward for it.

Let no corrupt communication proceed out of your mouth, but that which is good to the use of edifying, that it may minister grace unto the hearers.

Ephesians 4:29 KJV

In his book, *To Thine Own Self Be True,* Court Flint tells a story of a prominent woman invited to share before a large women's club the secret of her happy life. She told them a tramp was responsible.

She was washing dishes one morning when a tramp knocked at the back door, politely took off his hat, bowed and asked if he could work for breakfast. The woman said she told him in harsh tones, "I have no patience with tramps. I work for my living and you can work for yours. If you don't go, I'll call my husband." At that point the tramp said, "Your husband's not at home." She was startled and asked, "How do you know that?" He replied, "If he is home it's because he's sick. He wouldn't stay home with you unless he was sick."

This prominent, "happy" lady said she shut the door, unable to finish washing the dishes. Her thoughts went back over the morning when she had scolded her husband and had not been kind to him the evening before. The next day she asked God to help her change her life. She changed from a fault-finder into a "good-finder." A much happier marriage and an infinitely happier life was the result.

You get better results if you have high expectations. This is true in science, math, reading, football, or band.

—Charles Adair

The creation waits in eager expectation for the sons of God to be revealed.

Romans 8:19

In the early 1900s, Vilfredo Pareto, an Italian engineer-economist-sociologist, developed what he called the "80/20 rule." His research indicated that in a business 20 percent of the items accounted for 80 percent of the business and that roughly 20 percent of the population controlled roughly 80 percent of its wealth.

Since then others have incorrectly stated that "20% of the workforce contributes 80% of the results, and 20% of the sales force produces 80% of the sales." In most cases this is not true. At The Zig Ziglar Corporation in 1996, 20% of our sales people produced 25% of the business and 80% of our sales force produced 75%. In addition, our lowest-producing sales person produced 57% as much business as our top producer. This validates the fact that he is an extremely valuable employee. He served his clients well and made himself and the company a profit. As a result, we treat him with the same courtesy, respect, and dignity that we show all the other sales people. In short, he's a valuable employee and a first-class individual.

Treat everyone like they are top-drawer; show them respect and courtesy, and you'll be amazed at the number of them who will respond to your expectations and produce wonderful results.

Direction
literally creates
time.

The steps of good men
are directed by the Lord.
He delights in each step
they take.

Psalm 37:23 TLB

One day a traveler in a remote country town, convinced that he was on the wrong road, came to a halt in a village. Calling one of the villagers to the car window, he said, "Friend, I need help. I'm lost."

The villager looked at him for a moment. "Do you know where you are?" he asked.

"Yes," said the traveler. "I saw the name of your town as I entered."

The man nodded his head, "Do you know where you want to be?"

"Yes," the traveler replied.

"You're not lost," he said, "you just need directions."

Many of us are in the same position as that traveler. We know where we are—sometimes disappointed, dissatisfied, and experiencing little peace of mind. And we know where we want to be— at peace, fulfilled, and living life abundantly. Like the traveler, we are not lost—we just need directions.

It doesn't take much to find the high road to success, but to reach it you need an agenda for the present. You need directions for today. You need a purpose. Listen to the advice the president of Lincoln University gave to a group of incoming freshmen: "Your life can't go according to plan if you have no plan!"

When a job is loved, work makes life sweet, purposeful, and fruitful.

So I decided that there was nothing better for a man to do than to enjoy his food and drink, and his job. Then I realized that even this pleasure is from the hand of God.

Ecclesiastes 2:24-25 TLB

Many people look only at a problem and not at the opportunity which lies within the problem. For instance, two men looked out from prison bars—one saw mud, the other saw stars." That accurately describes two views of the world. Many employees complain about their job, not realizing that if the job were simple, the employer would have hired someone with less ability at a substantially lower wage.

Pessimism muddies the water of opportunity. For example, any time a new innovation came along promising to make life easier and people more productive, protesters always complained that it would throw people out of work.

In our own lifetime we have seen the advent of the computer. Initially it was believed that many people would lose their jobs because the computers could do so much more. It is true that some had to retrain to stay marketable. However, I think almost everyone would agree that computers have created jobs and improved our standard of living immeasurably.

The next time you catch yourself complaining about the difficulty of your job, ask yourself the question, "Is there an easier, better, faster, cheaper way of doing this?" Who knows, maybe out of the question will come an answer and some real benefits for you, because it benefits others.

Remember that productivity alone doesn't guarantee security. You must combine productivity with a consistent positive attitude and a team effort, whether you're looking for a job or looking to keep the one you have.

—Marvin Walberg

For as the body without the spirit is dead, so faith without works is dead also.

James 2:26 KJV

My wife and I recently checked into a nice hotel and immediately went to the restaurant for dinner. I explained to the hostess that we were both hungry and in a hurry. The lady pleasantly said, "No problem." Ten minutes later I asked a nearby waitperson if she could get someone to take our order. She smiled and said she'd be happy to. A moment or two later our waitress arrived. She was pleasant, enthusiastic, and brought water and menus with her. My first words to her were, "Thank you. We are in somewhat of a hurry and are really hungry." She said, "I'll take care of it right away." Nearly ten minutes later she returned and took our order.

At that point my wife and I jointly decided that we had to leave. The manager interceded and apologized profusely. We did not encounter a single person during our one hour-plus wait who was not courteous, friendly, and pleasant. Under the circumstances, we would have preferred to have someone who was just casually nasty—but efficient in delivering what we ordered—than someone who was pleasant and courteous but who did not bring our food. Message: Combine a pleasant, positive attitude with efficient service; your business will prosper.

Children pay more attention to what you do than what you say.

—Mamma Ziglar

*Train the younger women
to love their husbands
and children.*

Titus 2:4

Richard was the second-youngest of nine children. One Saturday afternoon, three days before Christmas, my mother was in her usual rush to get everything done. She asked Richard to go upstairs and polish her Sunday shoes. After awhile Richard brought down the shoes, obviously proud of the job he had done. Mother was so pleased that she reached into her purse and handed him a quarter. A quarter was quite a treasure, especially three days before Christmas, but Richard looked puzzled. He took the money, picked up the shoes, and quietly went back upstairs. In a few minutes, mother rushed up to change her clothes. As she slipped her feet into the shiny shoes, her right foot hit a lump in the toe. She was half-annoyed and hurriedly pulled out a wad of paper. She unwrapped it and out fell a quarter. Written in a seven-year-old scrawl were the words, "I done it for love."

—Margaret Baillargeon in *Catholic Digest*

Richard's parents had taught him the true meaning of love. Surely his mother, with nine children, was a busy lady. However, a wise and loving mother will find some time to spend with each child. Demonstrate your love to that little one, and you will help make a better world.

It is far more
important to be
the right kind of
person than it is
to marry the right
kind of person.

*Rejoice with the wife
of your youth.*

Proverbs 5:18 NKJV

Coming home on a plane, I noticed that the fellow seated next to me had his wedding band on the index finger of his right hand. I couldn't resist the temptation so I commented, "Friend, you've got your wedding band on the wrong finger." He responded, "Yeah, I married the wrong woman."

Many people have a lot of wrong ideas about marriage and what it takes to make that marriage happy and successful. I'll be the first to admit that it's possible that you did marry the wrong person. However, if you treat the wrong person like the right person, you could end up having the right person after all. On the other hand, if you marry the right person and treat that person wrong, you certainly will have ended up marrying the wrong person. I also know that it is far more important to *be* the right kind of person than it is to *marry* the right person. In short, whether you married the right or wrong person is primarily up to you.

Research, personal observation, and experience prove that stable, sound marriages are not built on the passion of the moment. Realistic (and positive) expectations lead to marriages that last.

You are the way you are because that's the way you want to be. If you really wanted to be any different, you would be in the process of changing right now.

—Fred Smith

I haven't learned all I should even yet, but I keep working toward that day when I will finally be all that Christ saved me for and wants me to be.

Philippians 3:12 TLB

If you've made a commitment to do something and you encounter difficulty, look for a solution to the problem. Without a commitment, you will look for an escape from the problem, and will generally find what you are looking for.

In all candor, there were long stretches of time when, despite my best efforts, I could not get a speaking engagement of any kind. That was discouraging, but not once did I consider abandoning my dream of being a speaker. The difference between me and many others who want to be speakers and have the necessary talent is that I never let go of my dream or the willingness to work toward achieving it. I had a dream, and the dream had me.

Most people who fail in their dream, fail not from lack of ability but from lack of commitment. Commitment produces consistent, enthusiastic effort that inevitably produces greater and greater rewards.

Motivation gives you the "want to." Training gives you the "how to," and the combination produces the necessary creative ideas to be more effective in realizing your dream. Commitment, discipline, and responsibility keep you going when the going gets tough.

The best thing
a parent can do for
a child is to love
his or her spouse.

Husbands, love your wives, just as Christ loved the church and gave himself up for her.

Ephesians 5:25

This reality was brought home to me when my son was about fifteen years old. We were taking a walk and I asked him, "Son, if anyone should ask you what you liked best about your dad, what would you say?"

He said, "I'd say that the thing I like best about my dad is that he loves my mom." Naturally I asked, "Son, why would you say that?" He replied, "I know because you love Mom you're going to treat her right, and as long as you treat her right, we will always be a family, because I know how much Mom loves you. That means, Dad, that I will never have to choose between you and Mom."

Talk to your kids about how great your spouse is. Tell them how much you love your spouse. Tell them how you met and what attracted you to your mate (You may need to remember this too!).

Knowing that you and your spouse love each other, gives your children a sense of security they cannot get any other way. They may try to find it elsewhere, but there's nothing like it. Let your kids know their parents love each other today!

Persistence is what makes the impossible possible, the possible likely, and the likely definite.

—Robert Half

We do not want you to become lazy, but to imitate those who through faith and patience inherit what has been promised.

Hebrews 6:12

The small boy's mother asked him a question: "What would you like to be and do most of all?" He looked at her and said, "I want to be big and I want to be athletic."

Unfortunately, that answer presented a serious problem. His mother, father and grandparents on both sides were all small in stature. His mother told him there might not be anything he could do about being big, but there was a great deal he could do about being an athlete.

For a long time it appeared that his mother was wrong on both counts, because the boy was clumsy. He was the last one chosen for any of the pick-up games, regardless of the sport. In the ninth grade his coach asked him why he continued to pursue the impossible dream of becoming an athlete.

For most boys this would have been a devastating blow, but the youngster the coach was talking to was Merlin Olsen. Not only had he started to grow, but he was developing the speed and coordination that enabled him to become an all-American high school football player. At Utah State he was an all-American defensive player and played in the NFL Pro Bowl fourteen times. Persistence pays!

The goal of many
leaders is to get people
to think more highly
of the leader. The goal
of a great leader is
to help people
think more highly
of themselves.

—John Maxwell

*But he that is greatest
among you shall be
your servant.*

Matthew 23:11 KJV

In a typical organization employing 100 people, roughly 8 of them do not "fit." Six of the 100 will be "super-stars" and will produce 8 times as much per individual as do the 86 remaining performers.

Obviously, these "super-stars" can't type 8 times faster or get 8 times as much work done. Their productivity comes from what they do, their attitudes and their relationships with other people. The "super-stars" are excited and make it a point to become well-informed on their jobs. They willingly share information with those who ask. They become mentors without thinking in terms of mentoring, only doing the right thing, fitting in, being helpful, and making their company a better one.

Why don't we hire more "super-stars"?

You can't hire them—you must develop them. That's the reason in our ever-changing society, with the dramatic increase in technology, an on-going training and personal development program is a must. Not only does it increase proficiency and competency, but it substantially reduces turnover.

For those companies that ask, "Why should I train my people and then lose them?", the answer is obvious: "One thing worse than training people and losing them is not training them and keeping them."

Caring is more
than compromise
and more than
mutual agreement
not to hurt each other.
It is a tacit agreement
to help each other.

—Anonymous

Carry each other's burdens,
and in this way you will
fulfill the law of Christ.

Galatians 6:2

One day when I was in the cookware business, I found that I had made more appointments than I could keep. I conducted dinner demonstrations that enabled us to sell cookware to the hostess and guests. We then delivered the cookware to the purchasers and taught them how to use it on their own stoves.

Since my mouth had made promises I couldn't keep, I asked my assistant, Gerry Arrowood, to help. I explained I wanted her to deliver the cookware to the six couples who had purchased from me that evening and teach them how to use it on their own stoves. Terror appeared in Gerry's eyes. Her hands shook as she said, "I can't do it!"

At first, I could not persuade her to change her mind. But on the way home, she gave it some more thought, and as she started to get out of the car she said, "Okay, I'll do it. You stuck your neck out, and I don't want to see it cut off."

The next night I got the most exciting phone call. Gerry said, "I don't ever remember having this much fun or feeling so good about myself. I'll be glad to do this for you anytime you want me to!"

Don't wait until you feel like taking a positive action. Take the action, and then you will feel like doing it.

What is faith? . . . It is the certainty that what we hope for is waiting for us, even though we cannot see it up ahead.

Hebrews 11:1 TLB

Remember my assistant Gerry? She helped me out of a bind by doing something she didn't really want to do. However, after taking that first step, she became highly motivated, and her self-image improved dramatically. Her confidence started to soar, her personality blossomed, and she became more assertive. She started setting bigger goals; her optimism rose; she became more positive. The results speak for themselves.

Let me point out that Gerry started with only courage, compassion, pride, and humility; she was conscientious, absolutely dependable, and a very hard worker. She developed other success qualities as a direct result of using what she already had. That's a tremendous lesson for you to learn about motivation!

Don't miss a major, major point. The motivation came after she took action. Lesson—don't wait until you feel like taking a positive action. Take the action and then you will feel like doing it. That's taking responsibility. And when Gerry did that, the picture she had of herself changed, and her life changed.

The same can happen for you. Don't wait any more for the feeling to hit you. The motivation will come after you take those first steps.

You cannot receive a sincere compliment without feeling better . . . and just as important, you cannot give a sincere compliment without feeling better yourself!

Pleasant words are a honeycomb, sweet to the soul and healing to the bones.

Proverbs 16:24

One of the most effective tools you can ever use to teach and motivate is a sincere compliment. The more sincere the compliment, the more effective it will be. Unfortunately, too many of us pass out those sincere compliments as if each one were skin off our backs. In our business, personal, and family lives, we continue to play the "Gotcha!" game. You come in at the end of the day, walking kind of proud, wearing your new coat and tie, and your loving spouse greets you at the back door. Her eyes grow large as she zeros in on your new attire and your proud bearing and she says, "Honey, I like your coat and tie . . . [pause] . . . hang on to them—I hear they're coming back in style." Gotcha!

Evidence is solid that even one nasty "gotcha" can do serious damage, and a continuous barrage of them can do irreparable harm and adversely affect an entire department.

Part of our hesitancy in sharing a compliment is the fear that it will be misinterpreted. Even though it would be sincere, we often don't share it because of the fear of being misunderstood. This results in two people losing. Sharing the compliment results in a double win!

The dollar bills the
customer gets from
the teller in four
banks are the same.
What is different
are the tellers.

—Stanley Marcus

*Her ways are ways of
pleasantness, and all
her paths are peace.*

Proverbs 3:17 NKJV

My dictionary tells me that personality is the "personal or individual quality that makes one person be different and act differently from another." Personality is "the total physical, intellectual and emotional structure of an individual, including abilities, interests and attitudes."

There are many benefits to having a pleasant personality. Unfortunately, many people have forgotten that we can choose to smile and be pleasant or to frown and be thoughtless. Regrettably, too many people make the wrong choice and, as a result, their personality makes them come across as someone we don't want as a friend or co-worker.

There is only one opportunity to make a first impression, and all of us instinctively make decisions or judgments about an individual within the first few seconds of crossing paths. With that in mind, I believe when we teach our kids to smile, to be pleasant and cheerful, to be courteous and respectful of others, to pleasantly respond to requests or questions, we are helping them develop a personality that will open many doors for them. Once the doors are opened, character will keep them open; but personality, not character, is on display in the first few seconds. Therefore, it's important to develop a pleasant personality and use it for life.

Efficiency is doing things right. Effectiveness is doing the right things.

—Thomas K. Connellan

A man is known by his actions.

Proverbs 21:8 *TLB*

The proper utilization of our time and resources involves some truths which are so simple and basic that many people miss them completely. We need to understand that there is no point in doing well those things which we should not be doing at all. When you take on a task, you should ask yourself if this is something you should be doing, or is it something someone else should be doing. Focus on effective use of time, rather than efficient use of time.

What happens to those effective people who take their jobs seriously and use their time wisely? According to an *Associated Press* release from a few years ago, they get promoted:

> Dull people may not be the first invited to parties, but they are usually the first in line for promotion, according to a research team at a medical college in Chicago. The team made a study of eighty-eight executives and found that those people with a "low pleasure capacity" make the most successful executives. This is because they can concentrate on their work without being distracted. . . . Executives who were categorized as "fun seeking" tended to have lower salaries.

That doesn't mean you're not a fun person. It just means you take your job seriously and do things effectively.

LOST—Somewhere between sunrise and sunset—one golden hour encrusted with sixty silver minutes, each studded with sixty diamond seconds. No reward is offered. They are lost and gone forever.

—Anonymous

Be very careful, then, how you live—not as unwise but as wise, making the most of every opportunity, because the days are evil.

Ephesians 5:15-16

My friend Dan Bellus is—in my judgement—the number one time-management authority in our country. He says this:

When the Colonists declared their independence from Great Britain, a statement was written: "All men are created equal." There has been a lot of discussion about the truth of that statement since the time it was written. I don't propose I can clear it all up, but this I do know—everyone is equal in the amount of time he or she receives.

Everyone gets twenty-four hours a day—sixty minutes for every hour and sixty seconds for every minute. No one can get more; no one can get less. You can't play the "army" game with time: if you know the guy who's handing out the chow you can say, "I want more." You can't build a bigger time pipeline and say, "I want more." No one can live more than one second at a time. In this sense, then, everyone is truly equal. Now this one fact alone makes time the most precious of all commodities. This factor forces us to an inescapable conclusion: We've got to make our time work for us—it's the most perishable and nonnegotiable possession we have. We have to get production out of every second.

What you do off the job plays a major role in how far you go on the job. How many good books do you read each year? How often do you attend workshops? Who do you spend most of your time with?

Study to shew thyself approved unto God, a workman that needeth not to be ashamed, rightly dividing the word of truth.

2 Timothy 2:15 KJV

A classic example of someone who hasn't finished her education is Laurie Magers. She has been my administrative assistant for years. She came to work with less than a high-school education, but she clearly understood that she could continue her education as she had already been doing from the moment she left school and went to work. She's an avid reader and a good student of vocabulary. She attends lectures and seminars on a regular basis, and has for many years.

When we conducted a comprehensive evaluation for the key people in our company, Laurie scored slightly higher than the master's level of education average. (A Georgetown University Medical School study revealed that in 100 percent of the cases when a person improved vocabulary, his or her IQ increased.) Because Laurie continued her education on the job and off the job, she has not only job security at our company, but employment security, should something happen to our company.

Your input determines your output. Read biographies of successful people, read training books that relate to your field. Attend workshops and seminars. Rub elbows with the leaders in your company. All those little things will add up to making you a better employee.

If you want to change
your life for the better,
you must start
immediately and
do it flamboyantly.

—William James

*Now your attitudes and
thoughts must all be
constantly changing for
the better.*

Ephesians 4:23-24 TLB

I am your constant companion. I am your greatest helper or heaviest burden. I will push you onward and upward or drag you down to failure. I am completely at your command. Ninety percent of the things you do might just as well be turned over to me, and I will be able to do them quickly and correctly. I am easily managed, show me exactly how you want something done and after a few lessons I will do them automatically. I am the servant of all great people and, alas! of all failures as well. I am not a machine, though I work with all the precision of a machine, plus the intelligence of a man. You can run me for profit or run me for ruin—it makes no difference to me. Take me, train me, be firm with me, and I will place the world at your feet. Be easy with me and I will destroy you. Who am I? I am Habit.

—Author Unknown

Good habits must be grabbed firmly, forcefully, with a strong commitment. Regardless of how you feel at the moment, any decision reinforced by your will to take action on your commitment, will produce some marvelous results in an amazingly short period of time.

You become great by doing small things in a great way.

Whoever can be trusted with very little can also be trusted with much.

Luke 16:10

Sometimes it's the things that don't take much time—a kind word, an encouraging thought, a courageous act or even a battle in a war—that can affect the course of history. In the spring of 1942 things were not going well in World War II for the Allies and America.

Then came those thirty seconds over Tokyo that made a difference. Lt. Col. Jimmy Doolittle led the attack of sixteen U.S. B-52s, and they struck not only Tokyo but four other cities as well. The net result was Tokyo reacted by pulling ships and planes closer to Japan, while extending its defense perimeter. This decision soon led to the Battle of Midway—a U.S. triumph that marked the turning point of the Pacific war.

There is little doubt this brilliantly-planned, audacious attack shortened the war by many months and saved countless thousands of lives. Yes, even things that take as little as thirty seconds make big differences. Each one of us can identify a kind word, a friendly smile, a cheerful greeting, a thoughtful favor, etc., that lifted our spirits and increased our effectiveness. Interestingly enough, when we spend our time doing those simple "little things" for other people, we create a win/win situation, and both parties benefit.

Sitting still and wishing makes no person great. The good Lord sends the fishing, but you must dig the bait.

But he who looks into the perfect law of liberty and continues in it, and is not a forgetful hearer but a doer of the work, this one will be blessed in what he does.

James 1:25 NKJV

When I entered the business world I started and spent sixteen years in direct sales. Early on I had to knock on a lot of doors—we called it "canvassing." I do not ever remember looking forward to knocking on that first door—or even the second, or the third. However, by about the fourth or fifth door I was getting into the swing of things and actually looked forward to getting to the next door.

The start was by far the most difficult thing for me. I finally took the advice of one of my early mentors, Mr. P. C. Merrell, who suggested I make an appointment with myself to knock on the door of my first prospect at exactly the same time each day. He then suggested I put it out of my mind until it was time to go the next day. This approach eliminated procrastination, worry, and decision-making. It was some of the best advice I ever received.

Not just for sales people, but for procrastinators in general, if you have anything of a disagreeable nature which you must do, make an appointment with yourself. Forget about it and then, at the appointed time, start the project. You'll get more done with less worry.

For good or ill
your conversation is
your advertisement.
Every time you open
your mouth you
let men look into
your mind.

—Bruce Barton

*Out of the abundance
of the heart the
mouth speaketh.*

Matthew 12:34 KJV

Two geese were preparing to start their journey southward for their annual migration when a frog asked if they would be willing to take him with them. The geese said "yes," but wondered how it could be done. The frog was very creative, so he produced a long but strong stalk of grass. He persuaded the two geese to hold each end while he clung to the middle by his mouth.

The unusual three-some took off and were making good progress when some men below, observing the strange sight, loudly expressed their admiration for their creativity and wondered aloud who had been clever enough to design it. When the frog heard them, his vanity got the better of him and he opened his mouth to shout, "It was I!" He immediately fell to the earth and was dashed to pieces.

Perhaps the oldest adage about keeping our mouths shut is "Keep your mouth shut and people will never know just how ignorant you are. Open it and you remove all doubt."

As in most things, there are some elements of truth in these words. However, think of what we would lose if nobody talked. Wisdom will provide us the answer as to when we should talk and when we should listen.

The secret of getting ahead is getting started.

Lazy hands make
a man poor, but diligent
hands bring wealth.

Proverbs 10:4

All of us have undoubtedly made the statement, "I don't feel like it," a number of times. This expression in this particular instance has nothing to do with whether or not we are having a coronary or a migraine. It has to do with something which we need to do and should do, but don't want to do; so we simply say, "I just don't feel like it."

There's been an on-going conflict between doing our own thing and not doing things we really don't want to do because we don't feel like doing them. But the question is, "Can we trust those feelings?" Looking at the physical, any of you who have ever participated in any athletic endeavor know there have been many occasions when you did not "feel like" going out for practice, but because you did not want to incur the wrath of the coach and face possible dismissal from the team, you grudgingly got prepared, went to the practice field, and resentfully started the routine. A few minutes after you got into action, you began to feel a little better, and the more action you took, the better you felt. Then you went all out.

The message is simple: Do it and you will feel like doing it.

Having your dreams
fulfilled is far more
therapeutic than
having them analyzed.

*I can do all things
through Christ who
strengthens me.*

Philippians 4:13 NKJV

On August 6, 1926, Gertrude Ederle became the first woman to swim the English Channel. Her time was fourteen hours and thirty-one minutes, breaking Charles Toff's record by two hours and twenty-three minutes.

There are lessons from Gertrude (Trudy) Ederle that need to be mentioned. In the field of human endeavor, most of the time those on the sidelines admonish the participant to hang in there and see it through. However, in Trudy's case, those accompanying her—her father, sister, newspaper men, photographers, and her trainer, William Burgess, an Englishman who had finally conquered the Channel after eighteen previous failures—were encouraging her to throw in the towel. She was frozen, exhausted, battered, and sickened by the eleven hours of effort, but she never complained or showed any signs of faltering. Three miles from her goal, the Channel was buffeting her furiously and at that point her father and trainer called on her to quit, lest she be injured. Soon after came her classic reply to echo around the world: "Quit? What for?" Trudy staggered ashore and into the history books.

There's an old saying "When the going gets tough, the tough get going." Trudy teaches all of us quite a lesson with her accomplishment.

When I see the "Ten Most Wanted" list I always have this thought: If we'd made them feel wanted earlier, they wouldn't be wanted now.

—Eddie Cantor

Therefore comfort each other and edify one another, just as you also are doing.

I Thessalonians 5:11 NKJV

tar Daily is a man who became prominent in England as a notorious, vicious killer, a hardened armed robber whose difficulty can be traced to his childhood. His teacher routinely called on him to stand and read a passage in front of the class. Unfortunately, Star was a very poor reader, self-conscious, shy and inhibited; and the harder he tried, the more he failed.

On one occasion he was having a particularly difficult time and open laughter erupted in the classroom. Even his sister buried her head in laughter and embarrassment. The teacher, too, was working at hiding her laughter when he turned to her for support. At this point, young Star Daily exploded in anger and threw a book against the wall, screaming as he left, "One day you will fear me. You will hate me, but this will be the last time you laugh at me." The rest—as the saying goes—is history.

The word "encouragement" means "to put courage into." It's the fuel that provides the support people need to pursue their dreams. When we encourage our children and others to pursue their dreams, we help propel them into success. And when you give encouragement, you will receive encouragement.

Our chief want in
life is someone
to inspire us to be
what we really
want to be.

—Ralph Waldo Emerson

*But exhort one another daily,
while it is called To day.*

Hebrews 3:13 KJV

When Thomas Edison was sixty-seven years old, his uninsured plant at Menlo Park burned to the ground. By the time the ashes had cooled, Henry Ford presented Edison a check for $750,000. He told him there would be no interest charged, and if he needed more, it was available.

At that time Henry Ford was a successful manufacturer, and Edison was recognized as the premier inventor in the country. Question: "Why was Mr. Ford so generous and compassionate?" Answer: "When Mr. Ford was a young inventor, Edison was busy working on an electric automobile when he learned that Ford was working on a gasoline engine for cars. He went to see him and asked him innumerable questions about how the car would function. When the visit ended, Thomas Edison said to Henry Ford, 'Young man, you are onto something. I encourage you to pursue it. It can revolutionize transportation in our country.'" It was later said that the encouraging words from Thomas Edison caused Ford to renew his efforts to build the gasoline engine.

What you and I do might not have that much significance, but then, we may never know. As someone once said, "It's always a good time to encourage others and do our good deed for the day."

Look at the bright side— no matter how old you are, you are younger than you'll ever be again.

Now also when I am old and greyheaded, O God, forsake me not; until I have shewed thy strength unto this generation, and thy power to every one that is to come.

Psalm 71:18 KJV

On this bitterly cold day in Dallas, Texas, my beautiful redheaded wife asked me to put a leaf in the dining room table in preparation for the company party we were having at our home. I went downstairs and spread the table in preparation for the leaf. Then she asked the question, "Does the pool need water?" I looked out, agreed that it did, and headed outside to turn the water on. It was frozen solid and I could not turn it on. I came back inside, promptly headed upstairs and continued with my writing. No sooner had I gotten seated when my wife called and asked me if I was going to put the leaf in the table. She was laughing pretty hard when she asked. I laughingly said I was planning on doing it later, since I was busy at the moment. I said this as I headed downstairs to do her bidding, then returned to my writing.

Question: "Do I have a memory problem, or am I too focused on finishing my objective?" Needless to say, I believe it was my focus and not my memory. Be good to yourself on the memory issue. Claim the positive aspects of your memory and work on the others.

As the earth revolves
around the sun,
so should our lives
also revolve
around the Son.

If you confess with your mouth, "Jesus is Lord," and believe in your heart that God raised him from the dead, you will be saved.

Romans 10:9

On July 4, 1776, thirteen isolated colonies declared their *independence* from Great Britain, an event that shook the world and changed the course of history. On July 4, 1972, I declared my complete *dependence* on Jesus Christ, an event which completely changed my own personal, family, and business life.

From that moment on, God looked past my faults and saw my needs. He immediately showed me that He could and would replace everything that was missing in my life, but that nothing could replace Him in my life.

One thing I stress, even though I claim July 4 as my "born again" day, I'm not certain that it actually happened that day. I am certain it happened during that weekend. For me, there was no clanging of bells or flashing of lights. There was a warm, solid feeling of complete confidence that God saw my heart, heard my confession of sin, and welcomed me into His Kingdom when I acknowledged Jesus Christ as Lord and Savior.

It's important that you understand this, because many people, maybe including you, never have that earth-shattering moment of ecstasy. If you don't or didn't, don't be concerned. You are not saved by a feeling, but by trusting God and accepting Jesus Christ as your Savior.

You can no more do God's work without God than you could have sunshine without the sun.

Make every effort to enter through the narrow door, because many, I tell you, will try to enter and will not be able to.

Luke 13:24

I met a man at a service station not long after I turned my life over to the Lord. As we visited, he noticed the "Fish and Seven" pin I was wearing. He commented that he knew what the fish meant, but was unfamiliar with the overlaid seven. I explained that the seven was to serve as a reminder to me that there are seven days in every week, and they all belong to the Lord. I explained that I had recently turned my life entirely over to the Lord and that it had made a dramatic difference.

He lit up like the proverbial light bulb and said, "I know exactly what you mean, because I just accepted Christ as my personal Savior and it has really made a difference in my life." He went on to say that for over fifteen years he had served as a choir director in one of the local churches but had not known Jesus Christ personally until very recently.

At the time I thought this was an isolated incident, but since then I've met many people who are so close and yet so far. Don't be one of those people! If your life is out of balance in this one area, you can't be truly successful.

The way you see yourself today will affect your performance today.

For we walk by faith, not by sight.

2 Corinthians 5:7 KJV

Unfortunately, many people feel "it's all over" when they are in the prime of life. A classic example occurred once when I was on a call-in radio talk show. One caller was a lady who said to me, "Mr. Ziglar, I'm fifty-five years old. I've never done anything with my life, and now it's too late. It's all over."

Having experienced conversations with many people in that category, I had accumulated some information which I knew would be helpful. I came back at her with, "Ma'am, at fifty-five you're just a spring chicken! As a matter of fact, does your mama know where you are?"

I asked the lady if she was honest and at least reasonably intelligent and if she was employed. She responded in the affirmative, so I then asked, "Do you generally get two or three times as much work accomplished on the day before you go on vacation as you do on ordinary days?" She laughed and admitted that she did. Then I said, "Ma'am, one simple step will make a dramatic difference in your future. Go to work every day and perform like you do on the day before vacation." You can do the same.

Men and women
are limited not by the
place of their birth,
not by the color of
their skin, but by the
size of their hope.

—John Johnson

May the God of hope fill you
with all joy and peace as you
trust in him, so that you may
overflow with hope by the
power of the Holy Spirit.

Romans 15:13

John Johnson was raised in Arkansas City, Arkansas. That was a real break, because it is an established but little known fact that Arkansas City, Arkansas is the geographical center of the world. You can start there and go anywhere in the world you want to go—and the maximum distance is just twelve thousand miles.

Mr. Johnson went less than two thousand miles from the tin-roofed shotgun house where he was born, but he did go far enough to live on Chicago's Gold Coast and next door to Bob Hope in Palm Springs, California. He has been listed as one of the four hundred wealthiest men in America.

You, too, are fortunate because regardless of where you live, you are in the geographical center of the world. You can go from where you are to anywhere you want to go, and I speak of far more than just a geographical location. To be fair, I must warn you that it is not an easy trip. There will be the inevitable hills and valleys before you can go over the top. However, if you will supply the "want to," the information you have at your disposal will supply the "how to."

Nothing will ever
be attempted if all
possible objections
must first be overcome.

*Things which are
impossible with men are
possible with God.*

Luke 18:26 NKJV

few years ago, I spoke to the faculty and student body at Hinds Community College in Raymond, Mississippi. In 1943 I attended the school and took a course in history under Coach Joby Harris that had a profound impact on my life. I was speaking that day in an effort to raise funds to establish "The Joby and Jim Harris Scholarship Fund."

The auditorium was packed, and people were standing at the back and along the sides of the room. I noticed there were seven vacant seats on the front row and five empty seats on the second row. After a few moments I pointed out the empty seats and encouraged them to "come on down."

"On the second row those five empty seats are in the middle, and you will have to climb over three or four people to get to them. However," I said, "that's the way life is. In most cases there are obstacles standing between you and those opportunities in life, but I just want you to know that front-row seats are available everywhere. There is plenty of room at the top—but not enough room to sit down."

Remember—front-row seats are available, but you must step up and claim them.

Important:
Until you commit
your goals to
paper you have
intentions that are
seeds without soil.

—Anonymous

*Write the vision, and make
it plain upon tables, that he
may run that readeth it.*

Habakkuk 2:2 KJV

Goal setting is demanding, which is one of the reasons only three percent of us have a goals' program. This is also one reason the rewards for those who have a program are so great.

If you don't have time to invest in establishing a goals' program, is it possible that you don't have time because you don't have a goals' program? In all probability lack of time always has been and always will be the problem.

Make the commitment to establish a goals' program now, and you will have more time in the future to do what you need to do and want to do.

Stop! Right now set aside one hour, and make the commitment to start before you turn out the lights tonight.

Remember, change starts when you take the first step, and without action there will be no progress.

If you begin developing your goals' program, you will create for yourself an additional two to ten hours of productive time every week for the rest of your life. And, when you learn how to set one goal, you will know how to set them all. It's also nice to know that a number of goals will involve several aspects of life and include goals within goals.

You get the best out of others when you give the best of yourself.

— Harvey Firestone

Serve one another in love.
The entire law is summed up
in a single command: "Love
your neighbor as yourself."

Galatians 5:13-14

Over the years I have frequently made the observation that anyone who could not get along with my wife has a problem. She is the most people-oriented, genuinely loving and caring person I have ever known. She has a rare capacity to establish rapport immediately and get on familiar ground soon thereafter. She has such a beautiful laugh, and her whole countenance lights up as she talks with people. This is true whether she's talking to a person who is struggling for survival or whether she's dealing with a celebrity.

This morning her love for people was emphasized when an immigrant who had told her he was going back to India presented her with a gift. The gift was inexpensive, but it spoke volumes about his appreciation to her for being kind, thoughtful, and considerate to him. She protested, but he just reiterated that her kindness and pleasantness to him made him simply want to give her a token of remembrance.

My wife and I just celebrated our fiftieth honeymoon and I can remember few gifts of any kind, value, or size which she has received with as much pleasure as this gift from an impoverished immigrant. She was genuinely moved. This genuine graciousness is one reason I love her and why she is so popular with everyone she meets.

Money will buy
all kinds of things
for my family, but it
won't buy their love.

For the love of money is a
root of all kinds of evil. Some
people, eager for money,
have wandered from the
faith and pierced themselves
with many griefs.

I Timothy 6:10 NIV

I confess that I was once like a young man who equated security with money and money with success. I was able to help him see where his perspective was off, because life had taught me that true contentment and total success come from the things money can't buy. Don't misunderstand. I like the things money can buy, and I'll bet you do, too. I like nice clothes, a beautiful house, big, comfortable cars, relaxing vacations, membership in a nice country club, and so on.

However, I love the things money won't buy. It will buy me a house, but not a home; a bed, but not a good night's sleep; pleasure, but not happiness; a good time, but not peace of mind; and a companion, but not a friend.

If you go for standard of living (money) first, you will probably earn considerable sums of money, but you will have no guarantee that your quality of life will improve. However, if you go for quality of life first, your standard of living will inevitably go up. With this approach you will arrive at the end of life's road with more of the things money will buy and far more of the things that money can't buy.

Kids go where there's excitement. They stay where there's love.

As arrows are in the hand of a mighty man; so are children of the youth.

Psalm 127:4 KJV

118

In 1924 Bill Havens was one of America's best rowers, and most people thought he would win three medals—probably gold—at the Olympic games in Paris. However, a few months before the Olympics, Havens realized that his wife was going to deliver their first-born child during his trip to Paris. Bill decided he could not leave his wife during this important time and forfeited his spot to another.

In 1952 Bill Havens got a telegram from his son, Frank, who had just won a gold medal in the 10,000 meter canoeing final at the Olympics in Helsinki, Finland. "Dear Dad: Thanks for waiting around for me to get born. I'm coming home with the gold medal you should have won. Your loving son, Frank." Bill Havens knew he had made the right choice.

One of the ironies of life is that many times parents work overtime or even take second jobs in order to provide their families with more of the "good things" in life. However, study after study has revealed that when given the choice, children for whom Mom and/or Dad are working so hard would prefer more of their parents' time. Your presence says more than a thousand gifts ever can, so parents, get your priorities in order.

No man ever got lost on a straight road.

—Abraham Lincoln

Make level paths for your feet and take only ways that are firm.

Proverbs 4:26

Several years ago there was a scandal involving Solomon Brothers because of some securities violations. The situation was so serious that many people feared they would be closed down by the government. The economic impact would have been astronomical. Mr. Warren Buffett, the largest individual stockholder in Solomon Brothers, entered the picture and persuaded the government agencies to "call off the dogs." Though he had not been active in the running of the company, he promised the government he would do so for at least a year until it stabilized.

One of the ironies of the case is this: The illegal actions by Solomon Brothers' representatives averaged earning them $250,000 for each incident. The ones they did in a legal and above-board manner netted them an average of $1.5 million. This reminds me of something my mother said to me many times when I was growing up. She pointed out that "the right way is always the best way."

Mr. Buffett always makes his investments not on the current price of the stock but on the current condition of the company's management. He knows that men and women build business, and if they are men and women of ability and integrity they will build a profitable business. Yes, integrity definitely pays.

Your attitude determines (establishes) your altitude, as you cannot go higher than you think you can.

Therefore, prepare your minds for action; be self-controlled; set your hope fully on the grace to be given you when Jesus Christ is revealed.

1 Peter 1:13

In his *Speaker's Source Book*, Glen Van Ekeren tells a fascinating story about Josh O'Reilly and the San Antonio baseball team which was a member of the Texas Baseball League back in the days when minor league baseball was really good. It seems that all nine of his starting players were batting over .300, and everyone figured they were a "shoo-in" for the league championship when suddenly disaster struck. The entire team fell into a slump.

Then O'Reilly heard about a traveling evangelist who was "capable of creating miracles." In a burst of inspiration, O'Reilly grabbed every baseball bat his team had, placed them in a wheelbarrow, and went off to see Rev. Slater. When he returned, O'Reilly announced to his team that each bat had been blessed by Slater, and they were now assured success. As a result, a miraculous turn-around occurred.

The irony, of course, is that no one ever knew with certainty whether or not Slater had even seen those bats. But suppose he had? What on earth could he have done to a baseball bat? I think you'll agree—nothing. But what could he do to the minds and attitudes of the players? Obviously, a great deal. Yes, attitude really does make a difference.

One definition of insanity is to believe that you can keep on doing what you've been doing and get different results.

For the turning away of the simple will slay them, and the complacency of fools will destroy them.

Proverbs 1:32 NKJV

On May 15, 1930, the first airline hostesses boarded planes with the following set of instructions:

1. Keep the clock and altimeter wound up.
2. Carry a railroad time table in case the plane is grounded.
3. Warn passengers against throwing cigars and cigarettes out the windows.
4. Keep an eye on passengers when they go to the lavatory to be sure they don't mistakenly go out the emergency exit.

As a frequent flyer, I can assure you that none of those instructions are carried by the modern airliners of today. Change is inevitable and, in many ways, change is necessary. Yes, it is stressful but then so is unemployment and bankruptcy—and that's what faces the person who is unwilling to change. Basically, I'm speaking of "growth change," not change just for the sake of change. When I speak of "growth change," I simply mean we're adding things to our knowledge base which we did not know yesterday.

The mind works very simply: The old information mixes in with the new, and the blend helps us come up with something entirely different. When people are learning and growing, their inner creativity enables them to make the changes in full stride.

When you choose to be pleasant and positive in the way you treat others, you have also chosen, in most cases, how you are going to be treated by others.

Do for others what you want them to do for you.

Matthew 7:12 TLB

One day my son, Tom, and I were headed home from Phoenix, Arizona. It was hailing and traffic was heavy. When we got inside the terminal building, there were 11,286 people (approximately), and most of them were upset!

When we first got in line at the gate, the agent was a fair-skinned blond, but by the time we were face-to-face with him, he was a flaming red-head.

As my son and I stepped up to get our boarding passes, I enthusiastically greeted the gate agent, as I generally do, with the words "Good morning. How ya doin'?"

The young man looked at me and with a heavy dose of sarcasm replied, "Compared to whom?"

I smilingly responded, "Compared to the individual who doesn't have a job, who doesn't have nice, warm clothes to wear, or a comfortable building to work in. And especially compared to those people who live in lands where there's no freedom of speech, travel, or worship. How ya doin'?"

Talk about change in a human being! He grinned so widely he could have eaten a banana sideways. He replied, "I'm doing much, much better—and thank you very much for reminding me." The young agent's change in attitude led to a dramatic change in his actions.

As long as you keep
a person down, some
part of you has to be
down there to hold
him down, so it means
you cannot soar as
you otherwise might.

—Marian Anderson

*Bear with each other and
forgive whatever grievances
you may have against one
another. Forgive as the
Lord forgave you.*

Colossians 3:13

One of the interesting quirks of life is that frequently parents, educators, employers, coaches, etc., will say to someone in their charge, "I'm going to tell you something for your own good." Then they'll proceed to say something bad to them.

Years ago Sidney Harris asked the question, "Isn't it strange this is what happens. We say to someone, 'I'm doing this for your own good,' and then do something bad to them." Then he pondered the question, "I wonder why it is that when we tell someone we're going to tell them something for their own good, why don't we go ahead and tell them something good for their own good?" Makes sense to me.

Don't misunderstand. I believe all of us need to have those "Dutch Uncle" talks from time to time, where somebody points out the errors of our ways. But the message is delivered in a way that makes us know our advisor really cares about us and what we're doing. In life there are millions of people who have gone farther than they thought they could, because somebody else thought they could. Chances are good the person who encouraged them, told them something good for their own good.

Motivation fuels
that attitude that
builds the confidence
necessary to sustain
the persistence.

You need to persevere so
that when you have done the
will of God, you will receive
what he has promised.

Hebrews 10:36

One football team is dominating another when a big break suddenly occurs for the losing team, and every athlete on the team instantly feels a sense of excitement, fueled by hope that turns to belief that they can—and will—win the game. They feel victory, and that feeling is reinforced by the look in the eyes of the opposing players, many of whom are thinking, *Uh-oh, here we go again!*

Life is that way. When we sense that something positive is going to happen, we're energized. When we fear we're going to lose, we are de-energized and tighten up with negative results. That's why motivation is important for good times and bad. That's the reason a person who wants to maximize life will deliberately schedule regular motivational input, just as surely as he will schedule putting food into his stomach.

The infusion or injection of a new idea, a confidence-building thought, or a concept that makes sense will energize you, and build momentum within you. You perform better and learn more when you're up, so that's the time to take out some motivation insurance. Getting back up when circumstances have given you some tough blows is crucial to making it to the next level.

Check the records. There has never been an undisciplined person who was a champion. Regardless of the field of endeavor, you'll find this to be true.

Like a city whose walls are broken down is a man who lacks self-control.

Proverbs 25:28

According to the dictionary, "discipline" means "to instruct or educate, to inform the mind, to prepare by instructing in correct principles and habits; to advance and prepare by instruction." Author Sybil Stanton says true discipline isn't on your back, needling you with imperatives. It is at your side, nudging you with incentives. These are better pictures, because they truly build hope for the future.

The great violinist Isaac Stern was asked, "Is talent born?" The question was in reference to an outstanding performance by Isaac Stern himself. He responded "yes," talent is born, but musicians are made. It takes an incredible amount of discipline, hard work, and talent to become a great musician. No matter how great the talent or the field of endeavor, unless the individual is personally disciplined, much of the potential will remain just that—potential.

Roy L. Smith says that "discipline is the refining fire by which talent becomes ability."

Former Secretary of Defense Donald Laird says, "You will get much more done if you will only crack the whip at yourself."

Tie discipline to commitment, and it becomes an irreversible decision that you will do today what most people won't so you can have tomorrow what most people can't.

Winning isn't everything but wanting to win is.

—Vince Lombardi

But thanks be to God, who gives us the victory through our Lord Jesus Christ.

1 Corinthians 15:57 NKJV

I love the story of Vince Lombardi, coach of the Green Bay Packers, and his player, Jim Ringo, the perennial all-pro center. He was a strict disciplinarian who was one of the winningest coaches in history. Above all, he was highly respected for his will to win and his ability to get the most out of his players.

In 1964 the salaries of players were dramatically less than those of today, and Lombardi did all the negotiating. In a nutshell, he said, "Here's the deal—sign it," and most of them did. Green Bay was a winning team and there were fringe benefits to playing for world champions. However, Ringo felt he deserved more than Lombardi would offer, so he brought an agent with him. When they walked into Lombardi's office, Lombardi said, "Excuse me, I've got to make an important phone call." A few minutes later Lombardi walked back in and said to Ringo and his agent, "Gentlemen, you are in the wrong room." Looking puzzled, they asked, "What do you mean?" Lombardi replied, "Ringo, you no longer play for the Green Bay Packers. You have been traded to Philadelphia."

Lombardi was decisive. When he made a decision he acted on that decision, and the results spoke for themselves.

You're not old until you have lost all of your marvels.

—Anonymous

The glory of young men is their strength: and the beauty of old men is the grey head.

Proverbs 20:29 KJV

As a "junior senior citizen," I frequently encounter some real delights at being a member of the fastest growing segment of our society. Since I'm seventy, I've actually had enough birthdays to be classified as a full-fledged senior citizen, but I have a wrong "attitude," according to the way people generally think about senior citizens. For example, I honestly believe that my career is in front of me, rather than behind me, and I have more energy at seventy than I did at forty-five.

When Bismarck was chancellor of Germany in the 1870s he observed that virtually all of his powerful enemies were men who were sixty-five years old or older. He persuaded the German legislature to pass legislation making sixty-five the mandatory age for retirement.

What an absolute tragedy to encourage people to quit when they are at the very peak of their intellect, wisdom, and experience! Could that be the reason that the only time the Bible mentions retirement it is as a punishment?

Winston Churchill initiated his protest against Hitler as Prime Minister at sixty-five, and on his eighty-seventh birthday a young reporter commented, "Sir Winston, I hope to wish you well on your 100th birthday." Churchill quickly replied, "You might do it. You look healthy!"

Watch your thoughts,

they become words.

Watch your words,

they become actions.

Watch your actions,

they become habits.

Watch your habits,

they become character.

Watch your character,

it becomes your destiny.

—Motto, Metropolitan Milwaukee YMCA

Fix your thoughts on what is true and good and right. Think about things that are pure and lovely, and dwell on the fine, good things in others. Think about all you can praise God for and be glad about.

Philippians 4:8 TLB

My friend, Rabbi Daniel Lapin, in his publication *Thought Tool*, gives us this valuable input.

If we listen as others are maligned, in spite of our disinclination to believe what we hear, our relationship with the vilified individual is forever altered. Listening to gossip will usually leave us feeling dissatisfied with our spouse, children, employees, friends, or life in general. Speaking gossip usually leaves us feeling less worthy. Words penetrate to our souls and cannot be erased or ignored.

Overcome your inhibitions about talking to yourself. Speak passionately to yourself. Prepare speeches by actually saying them out loud. A winning mind-set is the consequence of hearing words that penetrate right to the core of personality.

If we truly wish to believe something, we should tell it to ourselves audibly, rather than think it silently.

Since we remember far better that which we hear, reading aloud increases our vocabulary, fluency, and range of ideas. Above all, it inspires.

Each time you say something good about someone in your life, you increasingly believe it yourself.

Through speech one can substantially increase inner feelings of harmony and satisfaction with certain unchangeable facts of one's life. Praising God makes for a close relationship with Him. This is part of the basis for praying out loud.

There's harmony and inner peace to be found in following a moral compass that points in the same direction, regardless of fashion or trend.

—Ted Koppel

Blessed is the man who does not walk in the counsel of the wicked or stand in the way of sinners or sit in the seat of mockers.

Psalm 1:1

Senator Frank Carlson from Kansas wrote:

God and the world need men who will stand in the gap . . . men who are not for sale; men who are honest, sound from center to circumference, true to the heart's core; men with consciences as steady as the needle to the pole; men who will stand for the right if the heavens totter and the earth reels; men who can tell the truth and look the world right in the eye; men who neither brag nor run; men who neither flag nor flinch; men who can have courage without shouting it; men in whom the courage of everlasting life runs still, deep, and strong; men who know their message and tell it; men who know their place and fill it; men who know their business and attend to it; men who will not lie, shirk, or dodge; men who are not too lazy to work, nor too proud to be poor.

Senator Carlson described a great need in our country today. The exciting thing is that everything Senator Carlson has described can be taught. However, it needs to be taught at home, reinforced in the school room, implemented in the business community, and practiced in the political arena.

Outstanding people
have one thing
in common:
an absolute sense
of mission.

*For whatever is born of
God overcomes the world.
And this is the victory that
has overcome the world—
our faith.*

1 John 5:4 NKJV

James Usher, an African American lad who was born and spent his early years in Pontotoc, Mississippi, didn't know he had no chance in life. At twelve he was earning $160 a week cutting yards working with his best friend, Steve, who was caucasian and lived across the street. Steve's mother, Mrs. Colleen White, befriended James and was his benefactor in untold ways.

Despite the fact he was voted by his classmates the "least likely to succeed," today this bright, highly-motivated, articulate young man owns several businesses and is a motivational speaker and certified trainer. He provides scholarships for students and assists those who have financial needs. James is active in his church and is modest about his accomplishments. Years ago his objective was to become wealthy by age thirty-five so that he could devote the rest of his life to helping other people realize and accelerate their dreams.

One of James' major concerns is the negativism permeating much of his race. Too many have lost hope, and that's the reason he's committed to providing the training and encouragement that will make a difference in their lives. James Usher is an example for all of us.

No one can make you feel inferior without your consent.

—Eleanor Roosevelt

For we are God's workmanship, created in Christ Jesus to do good works, which God prepared in advance for us to do.

Ephesians 2:10

Filadelfio Rael was born on a poor ranch in New Mexico, and his schooling ended with third grade. As a child he worked for farmers and ranchers and sold wood he collected to help provide for his parents. When he married, he and Mrs. Rael had six children. Filadelfio worked hard at the local steel mill where his earnings were just enough to get by from week to week.

In August, 1969, he started cleaning yards. His first day of work, he brought home $35.00. For several years Filadelfio worked seven days a week to keep his business, Rael's Trash Service, going while working full-time at the CF&I Steel Corporation.

In 1996 a major explosion at the CF&I Steel Corporation severely injured Mr. Rael, but by then he had already relinquished his trash business to his sons and was raising horses. The doctors cautioned him to stay away from horses, because the severe burns he had suffered might become infected. However, today he enjoys roping and enters in parades for the joy he receives from his horses.

As a Christian, Filadelfio and his family give his faith credit for what he's been able to do. I might also add that his courage, hard work, and "never-say-die" attitude helped considerably.

Confrontation doesn't always bring a solution to the problem, but until you confront the problem, there will be no solution.

—James Baldwin

We will lovingly follow the truth at all times—speaking truly, dealing truly, living truly.

Ephesians 4:15 TLB

For several years the Miami Hurricanes of college football fame were the "bad boys on the block." Then they hired Butch Davis, the former defensive coordinator for the Dallas Cowboys, to lead the coaching staff. His people skills and coaching skills are superb. One of the first things he did when he arrived at the University, in addition to teaching the "x's and o's," was to start teaching character development, emphasizing that what the players did off the field had a direct bearing on how they performed on the field.

In the 1996 season Davis suspended eleven players, one of whom was an All-American and several others who were starters. This sent a clear message to the players on the team as well as to the high school seniors around America. Today many top high school players go to Miami because of the character emphasis Coach Davis has implemented. He tells his assistant coaches that in recruiting "they will be forgiven for making a talent mistake, but they will be fired for making a character mistake." He says, "There is no excuse for character errors."

He's preparing young men to win football games but, more importantly, he's preparing them for life. That's a great approach to take, Coach Davis.

It is more noble
to love the person
next to you than
it is to love
mankind in general.

*Beloved, let us love one
another: for love is of God;
and every one that loveth
is born of God, and
knoweth God.*

1 John 4:7 KJV

The key to building a happy, even romantic relationship with our mates is for us to understand that men and women are different. For example, ladies, you need to clearly understand that your husband does not care what's on television. All he wants to know is what *else* is on television.

The most important and romantic room in the house is any room other than the bedroom—the kitchen, den, study, or the laundry room. This is where friendship, relationships, and communication are established and you affirm that your mate is important to you and far more than just a sex object.

The fires of passion start out burning brightly but diminish over the years. However, the fires of friendship should increase more and more. I speak from fifty years of being married to the same beautiful, redheaded lady. Today we talk more and enjoy little things more than ever. This morning as she gave me a hug, she reminded me about the ice show which starts at 7:30 tonight. I immediately suggested we leave at five, assure ourselves of a good parking place, and have dinner together. She laughingly agreed and said, "Hey, that's a date!" That's the way you keep those romantic fires burning.

Success is knowing
the difference between
cornering people
and getting people
in your corner.

*Just as each of us has one
body with many members,
and these members do not
all have the same function,
so in Christ we who are
many form one body.*

Romans 12:4-5

The basketball accomplishments of Michael Jordan have been well documented by writers worldwide. However, most people overlook the fact that he is, and always has been, the consummate team player. He has great confidence in his ability to make the crucial baskets, doesn't think twice about asking for the ball in critical situations, and loves it when he's put to the test. But Michael has never hesitated when he was being double-teamed to pass the ball to an open teammate. His confidence in them enables the other players to also reach new heights.

A classic demonstration took place in the '97 playoff series between the Chicago Bulls and the Utah Jazz.

Perhaps the most significant play of the series took place in the waning seconds of the sixth game in Chicago. With five seconds on the clock, Jordan was guarded so he could not make a shot. Without hesitation he threw the ball to Steve Kerr who dropped in a seventeen-foot jump shot from behind the free-throw line for three points.

Jordan's confidence in Kerr was a determining factor in Kerr making the shot that ended the series. That's team play. We all need to remember that individuals score points, but teams win games.

The greatest good
we can do for others is
not to share our riches
with them, but reveal
their riches to them.

How much better is it to get
wisdom than gold! and to get
understanding rather to be
chosen than silver!

Proverbs 16:16 KJV

Many of you remember the movie *Stand And Deliver,* the story of Jaime Escalante, an immigrant from Bolivia who taught at Garfield High School in inner-city Los Angeles. He accomplished remarkable results with students known to be especially difficult to teach.

One story not depicted in the movie was the one about "the other Johnny." Escalante had two students named Johnny in his class. One was a straight A+ student, the other was an F+ student.

One evening at a PTA meeting, an excited mother approached Escalante and asked, "How is my Johnny doing?" Escalante figured that the F+ Johnny's mother would not be asking such a question, so he described in glowing terms the A+ Johnny. The next morning, Johnny—the F+ one—approached Mr. Escalante and said, "I really appreciate what you said to my mother about me, and I just want you to know that I'm going to work real hard to make what you said the truth." By the end of that grade period, he was a C-student; and by the end of the school year, he was on the honor roll.

If we treat others as if they were "the other Johnny," chances are dramatically better that they would, in fact, improve their performance.

It takes a character-based foundation to make good decisions which will impact us now and from now on.

My son, let them not depart from your eyes—keep sound wisdom and discretion; so they will be life to your soul and grace to your neck.

Proverbs 3:21-22 NKJV

The late singer/author Madame Ernestine Schumann-Heink struck a responsive chord with all of us when she wrote these profound words:

> Home is the first school and the first church for young ones, where they learn what is right, what is good and what is kind, where they go for comfort when they're hurt or sick; where joy is shared and sorrow eased. Where fathers and mothers are respected and loved; where children are wanted; where the simplest food is good enough for kings because it is earned. Where money is not so important as loving kindness. Where even the teakettle sings from happiness. That is home. God bless it.

Unfortunately, in today's world you will not find very many homes that fit that description. Many parents provide neither the shelter nor the guidance, love or care that give a baby a chance to become a happy, productive citizen in the future.

In addition to food, shelter, and clothing, children need love and affection. And by the end of the first year, parents and guardians should be reading to the child. Ethical, moral values should be taught at home from the beginning, because there are moral absolutes. With a solid character base to build on, our kids can be successful.

He who does not live in some degree for others hardly lives for himself.

—Montaigne

For you, brethren, have been called to liberty; only do not use liberty as an opportunity for the flesh, but through love serve one another.

Galatians 5:13 NKJV

The largest seminary in the world is Southwestern Baptist Theological Seminary in Fort Worth, Texas. However, there were some rough roads to be traveled along the way. During the depression years of the 1930s, finances were so short that no salaries could be paid. In September of that year, Southwestern's president, Dr. R. L. Scarborough, brought a report to the Southern Baptist Convention Executive Committee that was filled with emotion.

Dr. Scarborough said, "Brethren, we are through at Southwestern. For two years we haven't paid faculty salaries. Our percentage of the allocation will not see us through another year. Here is my resignation and I turn over to you the Seminary property."

After a few moments of stunned silence, Dr. Sempe, the president of Southern Seminary, arose and said, "I may lose my job for what I'm about to say. Southern Seminary has some income from endowments on which we can live. I move that Southern Seminary's apportionment be cut and the difference given to Southwestern." The unselfish compassion and cooperation averted a financial disaster, and a force for good was able to continue. That action taken nearly seventy years ago has had and will continue to have long-lasting effects. Apply unselfish action in all phases of your life.

If we express gratitude for what we have, we will have more to express gratitude for.

Sing and make music in your heart to the Lord, always giving thanks to God the Father for everything, in the name of our Lord Jesus Christ.

Ephesians 5:19-20

In his latest book psychiatrist Louis Cady makes this observation:

> Thanks For Nothing. Whether or not one believes in a Supreme Being, the notion that there is nothing to be grateful for outside of the self is, in my professional opinion, the first step down a very slippery slope to nihilism, despair, self-pity, isolation of the self, depression, and death.
>
> If we have nothing to feel grateful for, let us abandon gratitude for the miracle of new life which emerges every season as the trees and flowers bloom, and the cries of every newborn baby. If we have nothing to feel grateful for, let us abandon all love, respect, admiration and devotion to our parents who did the very best they could for us.
>
> If we have nothing to feel grateful for, let us state unequivocally that we care nothing for our marvelous bodies which, for most of us, carry us wherever we want to go and are capable of athletic mastery. Let us forget that with a moderate amount of exercise we can stay in finely-tuned shape and live a minimum of our three-score and ten years on this planet, enjoying our "holiday on earth."

Dr. Cady has reminded all of us of something to be thankful for.

To forgive is
to overlook an offense
and treat the offender
as not guilty.

Be kind to each other,
tenderhearted, forgiving one
another, just as God has
forgiven you because you
belong to Christ.

Ephesians 4:32 TLB

Forgiveness is dangerous. Many of you will look at that statement and wonder what's coming, because you've always been told that forgiveness is a must if your future is going to reach its full potential. And you're right—but the reason forgiveness is dangerous is that when others have badly used or abused you and you forgive them for doing it, you no longer have a convenient excuse for not succeeding in life.

Forgiveness is one of the most important steps you will ever take. Martha Thorilius put it this way: "How much more grievous are the consequences of anger than the causes of it?" Bill O'Hearn says, "We need to understand that in life we've been given so many BTU's of energy and that every time you love somebody and are nice to somebody you're given an extra portion of that energy."

Not only should we forgive but we need to develop a cheerful nature to go along with it. H. G. Wells tells us why: "While there is a chance of the world getting through its troubles, I hold that a reasonable man has to behave as though he were sure of it. If at the end your cheerfulness is not justified, at any rate you will have been cheerful."

If we were all perfect
there would be
no need for love
in this world.

My command is this:
Love each other as
I have loved you.

John 15:12

It's true that no one gets through the day or week, much less a lifetime, without someone with whom they live, work, play "dropping the ball." Their mate might forget to pick up the dry cleaning on the way home. The executive assistant forgets to give you the important message. Your mate slams the door and awakens the baby. Your teenager forgets to fill the gas tank.

How do you handle those little "boat-rockers"? The first thing you do is understand that the offending party, in all probability, had no malicious intent. They simply forgot. It could be they were distracted with a busy schedule or had neglected to make a note of it, not realizing the importance of the request and thinking it was "no big deal."

Next, put yourself in that person's position. Can you understand why or how they dropped the ball? Third, evaluate this in the context of the relationship. Does it really weigh much in the long-term relationship?

Finally, gently suggest to the offending party that while you realize it was not intentional, you would appreciate it if they would be a little more thoughtful in the future. Take this approach and your relationships will be more pleasant and longer-lasting.

If you're not generous
with a meager income,
you will never
be generous
with abundance.

—Harold Nigh

Give and you will receive. . . .
The way you give to others is
the way God will give to you.

Luke 6:38 NCV

Betty Noyce was from "away" as they say in Maine. She lived in Silicon Valley for over twenty years with her husband Robert, the founder of Intel Corp. When their marriage ended in 1976, she left with four children and $40 million. She went to Maine to heal and stayed to return the favor.

First, she gave her community a library and a golf course. Then, as both she and her fortune grew, she gave jobs. She wanted to donate $1 million to public television, but she didn't write a check. She built five houses, employing architects and carpenters, and donated the money from the sales.

At her memorial service, Owen Wells, her friend and lawyer said, "To be given a fortune and accept it not as a stroke of luck but a mission, as she did, represents a kind of moral fiber that is extraordinary."

"I just hope to make a little difference in my own community," she said. "Selfishly, I give where my donation will make my immediate environment safer, cleaner, brighter . . . I leave it to others to do as much as they can do in their communities. And that's the way the wider world improves." Betty Noyce was a difference-maker.

Make the most of yourself for that is all there is of you.

—Emerson

Do you not know that those who run in a race all run, but one receives the prize? Run in such a way that you may obtain it.

I Corinthians 9:24 NKJV

You had two parents and each of them had two parents, and they had a total of four parents. Before that, you had eight great-grandparents, sixteen great-great-grandparents, thirty-two great-great-great-grandparents. If you pursue that line and allow an average of 25 years between generations, that would simply mean that 500 years ago there were 1,048,576 people on earth involved in the production of you.

Now, if you calculate the average investment of time in you which has been expended by your parents, teachers, the farmers who raised the food you've eaten, and the workers who produced the automobiles you've ridden in, the numbers increase even more. Now add the schools, churches, office buildings, grocery and department stores, etc., in which you work and trade, combined with the workmen who paved the streets, the doctors who've cared for you, the dentists who've provided your dental care, authors who wrote books you've studied and read—the figures really get to be impressive.

When you consider it for a moment, you are the only one who can use the education and ability which all these people have contributed to you. You have an awesome responsibility to make their investment pay off, don't you?

Many who aspire to leadership fail because they've never learned to follow. They are like boys playing war in the street, but all is quiet. When you ask, "Is there a truce?" they respond, "No, we are all generals. No one will obey the command to charge."

—J. Oswald Sanders

Be ye followers of me, even as I also am of Christ.

1 Corinthians 11:1 KJV

Cal Ripkin has a dad who took an intense interest in him and taught him much of what he knows about baseball. When his dad was playing baseball he was gone from the family a great deal, but when he was home he spent a lot of time with his boys. He quickly understood that "through baseball I could get the most time with my dad." When his dad went to baseball clinics on Saturday mornings, Cal went with him.

Cal gives his dad credit for his work ethic and his will to win. He recalls the day he decided to clean his dad's car without being asked. When his dad saw what he was doing, Cal said, "It was one of those moments when you connect between a father and son. He was proud of me for taking the initiative." Cal says, "I remember seeing that special look on his face, which I also saw many times when I hit home runs and came around the bases."

What too many of us fail to recognize is that all of us are role models, that people are also watching us. When we become good role models, it means we ourselves are winning at the same time.

Today be aware of
how you are spending
your 1,440 beautiful
moments, and
spend them wisely.

Why, you do not even know
what will happen tomorrow.
What is your life? You are a
mist that appears for a little
while and then vanishes.

James 4:14

At the beginning of each year you have 525,600 minutes in your bank account. The major question is, "What use will you make of all of those minutes?" Needless to say, you're not guaranteed any of them, but what are you doing with the ones you have at this precise moment?

How many times have you told someone or been told by someone, "I just don't have any time!"? We repeatedly hear that couples are busier than ever and have less time for each other and their families, despite the fact that we currently have more labor-saving devices than any people in history. On the other hand, in many third-world countries, particularly in the interior, there are few, if any, watches, but they seem to have plenty of time.

Why do we say we "have no time" when, since the beginning of time there have been twenty-four hours in everybody's day? Could it be that we're not using our time wisely? It is true that if we don't plan our time, somebody else will take it. I'm confident you've noticed that people with nothing to do, as a general rule, want to do it with you. The message is clear: Organize. Establish your priorities. Follow them to the best of your ability.

Denial is not a river in Egypt; denial is ignoring the obvious.

Hear, ye deaf; and look, ye blind, that ye may see.

Isaiah 42:18 KJV

Since the beginning of time man has made every effort to "beat the system" or "get by with" what they can. Many people believe "it's easier to get forgiveness than it is to get permission." A classic example of this took place after the April 27, 1989, mandatory use of seat belts went into effect.

Entrepreneur Claudio Ciaravolo, a psychiatrist in Naples, Italy, cashed in big-time on the mandatory seat belt law. He invented a "security shirt," which was simple in design and devious in concept. It was a white tee-shirt with a diagonal black stripe designed to deceive the police into believing the motorist wearing it was buckled up.

Dr. Ciaravolo and the motorist had "fooled the law," but ultimately they fooled no one but themselves, and with the first collision the foolishness of their approach was revealed.

Remember when the size of a box of goods, whether soap, cereal, or candy, was an excellent indication of the volume of the contents? Unfortunately, this is no longer true. The inevitable result is a disappointed customer and, in many cases, that customer turns into an ex-customer. It's safe to say that those who "play it straight" ultimately benefit the most.

When obstacles arise, change your direction to reach your goal, not the decision to get there.

We are perplexed because we don't know why things happen as they do, but we don't give up and quit.

2 Corinthians 4:8 TLB

Many people have accomplished great things because they didn't know it couldn't be done. Henry Ford was broke at age forty, had limited formal education, but was a man with a vision. Mr. Ford conceived the idea that a v-8 engine was a possibility. His engineers scoffed at the idea. But since he was the boss, they halfheartedly worked on some plans before they told him it was an impossibility. Mr. Ford, however, insisted that the men give it more effort. They did, but still arrived at the same conclusion: Impossible. When they again told Mr. Ford that it was impossible, he came reasonably close to losing his temper and told the men in no uncertain terms that he had to have a v-8 engine. This time the men attacked it with new vigor and the v-8 engine became a reality.

How many times have we become convinced that something cannot be done, and then someone who doesn't know it can't be done adds a little wrinkle and gets it done?

Mr. Ford had an idea that was new, and yet common sense dictated that it would work. When you come up with "wild" ideas, engineer them properly and, who knows, maybe you will discover that you're a young Henry Ford in the making.

Your mind
acts on what
you feel it.

*If there be any virtue, and if
there be any praise,
think on these things.*

Philippians 4:8 KJV

everal years ago an article in the *New York Times* pointed out that many people have every reason to be negative about themselves and their lives. If they were poverty-stricken as a child, had been abused and neglected, felt no love and had never had a word of encouragement, etc., then "no wonder they are negative."

What can you do if you fit into that category? First, you accept the fact that failure is an event, not a person; that yesterday really did end last night, and today is a brand-new day. Second, you need to understand that you are what you are and where you are because of what's gone into your mind. When you change your thinking you change your actions; when you change your actions you change your future.

So the question is, "What do you put in your mind?" Make it a point to read books that are optimistic and upbeat. Attend seminars with other upbeat, optimistic people. Listen to motivational and inspirational cassette recordings in your car. In a matter of days your thinking will slowly, but perceptibly, start to shift. In a matter of months you will be strongly headed in the right direction with goals carefully written down and a good chance for reaching them.

Education and intelligence are not the same thing.

Determination to be wise
is the first step toward
becoming wise! And with your
wisdom, develop common
sense and good judgment.

Proverbs 4:7 TLB

The original version of a mutual fund prospectus:

Maturity and duration management decisions are made in the context of an intermediate maturity orientation. The maturity structure of the portfolio is adjusted in the anticipation of cyclical interest rate changes. Such adjustments are not made in an effort to compute short-term, day-to-day movements in the market, but instead are implemented in anticipation of longer term, secular shifts in the levels of interest rates (i.e. shifts transcending and/or not inherent to the business cycle).

The Warren Buffet version of the same mutual fund prospectus:

We will try to profit by correctly predicting future interest rates. When we have no strong opinion, we will generally hold intermediate-term bonds. But when we expect a major and sustained increase in rates, we will concentrate on short-term issues. And, conversely, if we expect a major shift to lower rates, we will buy long bonds. We will focus on the big picture and won't make moves based on short-term considerations.

Question: "Which explanation would you respond to first?" Isn't it true that most of us are inclined to take action only on what we understand? Just remember that anything which can be misunderstood will be misunderstood.

The most destitute
person in the world
is the one
without a smile.

For this very reason,
make every effort to
add . . . godliness, brotherly
kindness; and to brotherly
kindness, love.

2 Peter 1:5-7

A Smile

This is a story, a story of regret
I write this tale so you won't forget
A tale of a broken heart
past o'er time after time
'Til one day it decided it had had enough
It wanted to leave all the pain behind
No person would share their love
Not even a little touch
No one would ever give a smile
Just a smile, but it meant so much
if anyone had she would have gone on living
but I was too busy, that was my reason
This heart had walked three miles
Looking longingly just for one smile
She stopped at a bridge
No smile to be found
She calmly looked down
Soon death would come round
The very next day
That dear heart was found
it was smashed in the sea
Within it, no trace of love could be found
all that heart needed was a smile
But hundreds of people passed by her all that while
I often see that girl's face in my dreams
What if a smile on my face to her had been seen
but it wasn't—
I just looked down with a frown
What could I have done with my friends all around?
Could I have helped that girl not to drown?
All she wanted was a smile—
A smile that I am now happy to give
A smile I shall share as long as I live.

—Anne Sherman

Courage is not the absence of fear; it is going ahead despite the fear.

Be strong and courageous; do not be afraid nor dismayed before the king of Assyria, nor before all the multitude that is with him; for there are more with us than with him.

2 Chronicles 32:7 NKJV

Those of you who are fight fans and have seen Evander Holyfield in the ring will probably be stunned to learn that until he was seventeen years old he had a considerable fear of boxing.

Early in his career, as a slender hundred and forty-seven-pounder, he was decked with a left hook. But he got back up and tore into his opponent with fury. Later he had a dream about the incident and realized he had suffered no pain. In fact, he had actually felt slightly euphoric from his counter attack. From that moment on, Evander Holyfield had no fear of getting hurt.

This, in part, explains his utter lack of fear in facing Mike Tyson. However, Evander Holyfield, a man of great faith, is a disciplined fighter. He lives a clean life, trains exceptionally hard, listens to the advice of his trainers, and has developed the ability to punch and take a punch. In his first Tyson fight, Holyfield took Mike Tyson's best shots early and delivered even better shots in return, winning the championship.

Interesting, isn't it, that Holyfield's career really started after he had been knocked down. When we get "decked," we need to use it as a springboard to get up and climb to greater heights.

If you learn
from a defeat,
you haven't
really lost.

Give instruction to a wise
man, and he will be still
wiser; teach a just man,
and he will increase
in learning.

Proverbs 9:9 NKJV

A few years ago, Cal Ripkin, the shortstop for the Baltimore Orioles, signed a five-year contract for over $30 million. However, the previous year, Cal got only about one hit for every four times he stepped to the plate. Now let's think together about this for a moment. If you had failed three times out of four in your primary job, how would you feel about it? What would your self-image or picture of yourself be?

What do you think Cal Ripken's picture of himself is when he steps up to the plate? Do you really think that he's thinking, *Boy, what a waste of time! Chances are only one out of four I'm going to get a hit!* Do you think that's his self-talk? Then what is his self-talk?

I believe as he steps to the plate with considerable eagerness to face the pitcher, Cal is thinking to himself, *Okay, you got me the last time, but I've got your number this time. I've been thinking it through, watching you, and I happen to know I'm one of the best athletes in the world. This is my turn!*

Cal Ripken sees himself as a winner, and he is elated that he now has a chance to step back up to the plate.

Go as far as you can see, and when you get there you will always be able to see farther.

I press on toward the goal to win the prize for which God has called me heavenward in Christ Jesus.

Philippians 3:14

One evening in Sacramento, California, Richard Oates was scrounging around for quarters to feed the washing machine and clothes dryer when a thought suddenly hit him: *I've got too much ability to be in this situation.*

The next day he went to a small home builder and applied for a job. He was hired to clean out just-completed houses. That first day he did more than two men normally did, and his employer asked if he knew anything about finishing. He replied that he did. The next day he did more finishing in one day than two men generally do and was offered a full-time job. After a year he got a job with Ryland Homes. In a matter of about only three years he was a superintendent. His desire, along with that of his wife, my daughter Cindy, to live in Dallas moved them back here, and today he's doing a marvelous job as our chief operating officer.

I doubt seriously Richard had that as his objective when he was scrounging for those quarters, but the important thing about the success journey is that it starts with a thought which leads to action. When you do each thing full-speed ahead with the best of your ability, doors open.

Sign on the wall of a Baltimore church: "Trespassers will be prosecuted to the full extent of the law. Signed, The Sisters of Mercy."

How different from this way of faith is the way of law which says that a man is saved by obeying every law of God, without one slip.

Galatians 3:12 TLB

All of us have encountered the "these are the rules, we've always done it this way" type mentality in various business and governmental organizations. Perhaps the most extreme example of bureaucracy in full force I've heard of occurred when a distinguished-looking gentleman wearing blue jeans walked into a bank and sought to complete a transaction. The teller apologized, but explained it could not be done because the man who handled these particular transactions was out for the day. So he would need to return the next day. Since that was the only business the gentleman had in mind, he prepared to leave by asking the teller to validate his parking receipt.

The teller politely but firmly told him that their bank policy did not permit the validation of parking without the customer making a financial transaction. The man sought an exception, since he had come to do business, but the appropriate personnel was not available. She said, "I'm sorry, but that's our policy." Disturbed by her relentless legalism, the man then completed a transaction. John Acres, then chairman of IBM, withdrew all $1.5 million from his account. He left the bank with his validated parking ticket, and one teller left with a resolve not to be so legalistic at her next job.

Wouldn't it be
wonderful if our
mind growled like
our stomach does
when it is hungry?

*Prepare your minds
for action.*

I Peter 1:13

One of the most reliable and extensive sources of information comes from the materials we read. We have access to some of the greatest minds in the world in any field in which we have an interest. We can read the brilliant men and women who have gone before us and who are still living with us. The question is, "Do we take advantage of this incredible resource?"

Unfortunately, the answer for well over half of our people is "no." Fifty-eight percent of all people in our society, when they finish their formal education, never read another meaningful book. That's unbelievably tragic and limiting. On the other side of the scale, those who make "Who's Who in America" read an average of twenty meaningful books in a year. Obviously, in five years they will have read one hundred books by authorities in many different fields. Not only does this give them information, but it also provides inspiration and keeps them on the "grow." In short, these are mature, progressive, successful, happy, healthy people. Obviously, this is not always true, but give me 100 readers vs. 100 non-readers and when you chart the courses of their lives, I can assure you that the readers are more successful in every area of life.

Happiness is like a kiss. In order to get any good out of it, you have to give it to someone else.

Whatever a man sows, that will he also reap.

Galatians 6:7 NKJV

This last Valentine's Day I gave my wife, who has an absolute passion for them, some colorful foil-wrapped chocolate-covered marshmallows.

I gave her one by simply leaving it in plain view and, as always when we play this little game, she laughed because she knew the search was on. I hid the rest of them in places she periodically visits—the rice canister, the freezer, her dresser drawer, in items of clothing, etc.

The neat thing about this simple little inexpensive gift is that for at least the next three weeks I will hear her beautiful laugh as she uncovers another goodie. This candy comes in such small portions that eating it doesn't violate her diet too much, and the enjoyment both of us receive from the game is considerable. Invariably, if she makes a discovery when I'm at home, she will come give me a hug. Last November she and I celebrated our fiftieth honeymoon and, since we will continue to play games like this if we're both still here, we will someday celebrate our sixtieth and then our seventy-fifth wedding anniversaries. I believe if all married couples played little games like this, there would be more Golden Anniversaries celebrated.

A well-developed sense of humor is the pole that adds balance to your steps as you walk the tightrope of life.

—William A. Ward

A merry heart maketh a cheerful countenance.

Proverbs 15:13 KJV

194

One of my favorite anecdotes is the one I tell about going to the recreation center to do my exercising and weight lifting. I frequently point out that I had to cut down on the weight lifting, because I was bulking up so much that many people thought I was on steroids. As a general rule, that gets quite a good laugh, and when at age seventy, I tell this story, it is funny. However, if a young, husky, healthy thirty-year-old were to use this example, it would not be funny.

The same is true with ethnic jokes. Jews can tell jokes about fellow Jews, and everybody laughs at the story. Some of us can joke about "Bubba" and people will laugh, but when someone outside of those circles tells jokes about those inside the circle, it comes across as "racist" and insensitive. The same is true when we tell certain stories about members of the opposite sex.

The point is that everyone enjoys a good joke, but we must be careful to tell the joke in good taste and make certain we are not being sexist, racist, or prejudiced in any way. Think about that as you use humor, and it will help you in your climb to the top.

You Know You're at the Top When …

1.

You've made friends
with the past, are
focused on the present,
and optimistic about
your future.

*Forgetting what is behind
and straining toward what
is ahead, I press on toward
the goal.*

Philippians 3:13-14

At the end of the 1996 basketball season, Michael Jordan was the proud possessor of two more MVP trophies. He earned one for regular season play and one for the championship series.

He had made it back and had shaken off the "rust" he had accumulated during the eighteen months he spent playing baseball in the minor leagues. However, there's more to the story. When he decided to rejoin the Chicago Bulls during the last portion of the 1995 season, he was confident he could quickly return to form. Admittedly, there were occasions when he showed flashes of brilliance on the court, but much of the time he struggled. Then, his return to glory was thwarted by the Orlando Magic in the semifinals.

The disappointing experiences took their toll on Jordan who said, "The disappointments of last year motivated me to bounce back," and he even thanked the Orlando Magic for giving him the incentive. He used the adversity of defeat as a catalyst to train harder in the off-season. This year he is back on top of his game, and he is again the premier player in basketball.

Welcome back, Michael. You inspire all of us to give life "one more shot" and prepare better for it in the process.

You Know You're at the Top When . . .

2.

You have made
friends of your
adversaries and have
gained the love and
respect of those who
know you best.

But I say unto you which
hear, Love your enemies,
do good to them which
hate you.

Luke 6:27 KJV

busy executive was being pressured by his seven-year-old son to pay attention to him, and the father kept putting him off. In one last effort for attention, the youngster said, "Dad, who do you like best—Batman or Superman?" The father impatiently replied, "Oh, I don't know. I suppose Superman." His son persisted, "Dad, aren't you going to ask me who I like best?" The father answered, "Oh, all right, Son, who do you like best?" The boy said, "I like Batman best." The father simply commented, "Well, that's nice," and went back to his work. Then with a pleading tone in his voice, the little boy said, "Dad, aren't you going to ask me why I like Batman best?" "O.K., Son, why do you like Batman best?" The youngster replied, "Because Batman has a friend." With that, the father put aside his work, looked at his son and said, "Having a friend is really important, isn't it, Son?" And the youngster responded, "Yes it is, Dad."

This little story says something to all of us, doesn't it? I've never yet met anyone who would not, when pressed, admit that they really treasure friendships. The need for human companionship is present in all of us. We want someone we can call "friend."

You Know You're at the Top When . . .

3.

You are filled with
faith, hope, and love
and live without
anger, greed, guilt,
envy, or thoughts
of revenge.

And now these three remain:
faith, hope and love.
But the greatest of
these is love.

1 Corinthians 13:13

My opthamologist, Nathan L. Lipton, M.D., P.A., goes the "extra mile" with each eye examination and gives me a complete print-out on the condition of my eyes. He also includes some wise advice about life in his evaluation. For example, my most recent report included these gems:

> This year think first of someone else.
> Take pleasure in the beauty and wonder of the earth.
> Write a love letter. Share some treasure.
> Gladden the heart of a child. Welcome a stranger.
> Thank God for what you are and what you have,
>   whether it be great or small.
> Mend a quarrel. Give a soft answer.
> Seek out a forgotten friend.
> Dismiss suspicion, and replace it with trust.
> Keep a promise. Find the time.
> Forego a grudge. Forgive an enemy.
> Apologize if you were wrong.
> Listen. Try to understand.
> Examine your demands on others.
> Appreciate. Be kind; be gentle.
> Laugh a little. Laugh a little more.
> Love completely. Speak of your love.

These are but inklings of a vast category, a mere scratching of the surface.

They are simple things; you have heard them all before; but their influence has never been measured.

This year, they can all change your life.

You Know You're at the Top When ...

4.

You know that failure to stand for what is morally right is the prelude to being the victim of what is criminally wrong.

Watch, stand fast in the faith, be brave, be strong.

1 Corinthians 16:13 NKJV

Our company has a course called "I CAN," which teaches commitment, honesty, enthusiasm, responsibility, the right mental attitude, and other positive characteristics. Charlie Pfluger, an assistant principal from an inner-city school in Indianapolis, Indiana, attended one of our seminars and recognized the benefits that would come to his school if these things were taught to the kids.

They initiated a program to give the kids an "I CAN" dollar every time they were seen doing something unusually good or helpful. If they were seen helping a senior citizen across the street, picking up trash on the school grounds, erasing the blackboards, or enthusiastically welcoming a newcomer to school, they would get an "I CAN" dollar. A hundred of them procured a "Winner's" T-shirt.

Of the 593 kids in that inner-city school, 587 won the "Winner" T-shirt. Five hundred eighty-seven T-shirts might be considered expensive, but the rest of the story is this: There was not one single incidence of violence or vandalism, no drug arrests, grades improved and since "I CAN" teaches kids to thank their parents for something nice they did that day, for the first time teachers, students, and parents united in their common objective. When kids learn these principles, they are learning things that will prepare them for life.

You Know You're at the Top When ...

5.

You are mature enough to delay gratification and shift your focus from your rights to your responsibilities.

But let patience have her perfect work, that ye may be perfect and entire, wanting nothing.

James 1:4 KJV

All of us have awakened on a given morning, not really "feeling" like going to work. However, being a responsible individual, we roll out of bed, head for the kitchen for a cup of coffee, and in the process realize that we probably are going to survive. We get dressed, drive to work, and when we show up, we pitch in. Two hours later we actually feel good. The action produced the feeling.

Don't misunderstand. I'm not suggesting that if you're suffering from a coronary or if you underwent major surgery yesterday you should get up and go to work. That would be ridiculous. What I am saying is that many times when we are slightly "out of the mood" for doing a job we fabricate a few symptoms of simply not feeling well, and if we're not careful, we indulge in a little self-pity and decide to pamper ourselves.

Message: Responsibility and commitment are key elements in meeting obligations. The responsible individual who has made a commitment to do a job or perform a task is going to follow through on the commitment to fulfill his or her responsibility. That's a major key to success in personal, family, and business life.

You Know You're at the Top When …

6.

You love the
unlovable and give
hope to the hopeless,
friendship to the
friendless, and
encouragement to
the discouraged.

*A man who has friends
must himself be friendly.*

Proverbs 18:24 NKJV

Henry Lebow tells the story of buying a new television set. "The neighbors gathered one Saturday to help us put up the antenna. Most of them had only the simplest tools, so they weren't making much progress. Then one of the neighbors who was new on the block appeared with an elaborate tool box. The box contained everything needed to get the antenna up in record time." Henry said that as they all stood around congratulating themselves on this piece of good luck, they asked the new neighbor what he made with such fancy tools. The new neighbor smiled and answered, "Friends, mostly."

What a marvelous example and illustration! Wouldn't it be wonderful if each of us thought in terms of making friends by doing such simple acts as this to make those friends? Perhaps it's taking a meal to a shut-in. Or if there's been a death in the family take some prepared food to the grieving, so the survivors won't have that additional burden on their hands.

The best way to make friends is to be friendly. It can start with a simple smile, a cheerful "hello," or a word of encouragement. It's amazing what an impact you will have when you engage in a kind word or simple, thoughtful act of kindness.

You Know You're at the Top When …

7.

You know that
success doesn't
make you, and failure
doesn't break you.

*Forgetting what is behind
and straining toward what is
ahead, I press on toward the
goal to win the prize for
which God has called me
heavenward in Christ Jesus.*

Philippians 3:13-14 NIV

Failure can and should be a motivator. Dr. J. Allan Petersen said it best. "Everyone, at one time or another, has felt like a complete failure. Many have allowed the fear of failure to destroy them. Actually, fear is far more destructive than failure and in any area of life, fear of failure can defeat you before you get started."

What makes us so afraid of failure? It's worry about what people think. "What will they say?" we ask, as if it were the ultimate scandal to fail. We assume that because we've made one or several mistakes, we're failures and therefore forever disgraced. What a ridiculous assumption! How many people are completely successful in every department of life? Not one. The most successful people are the ones who learn from their mistakes and turn their failures into opportunities.

A failure means you've put forth some effort. That's good. Failure gives you an opportunity to learn a better way to do it. That's positive. A failure teaches you something and adds to your experience. That's very helpful. Failure is an event, never a person; an attitude, not an outcome; a temporary inconvenience; a stepping-stone. Our response to it determines just how helpful it can be.

You Know You're at the Top When …

8.

You are at
peace with God
and man.

Therefore being justified by faith, we have peace with God through our Lord Jesus Christ.

Romans 5:1 KJV

Does "faith" and/or "religion" work? Is it effective? A study conducted in 1988 by Dr. Randolph Bird, a cardiologist at the University of California at San Francisco School of Medicine, emphatically says "yes." Dr. Bird tested the impact of distant prayer, much like a new medication. He recorded its effects on nearly 400 patients who all had severe chest pains and/or heart attacks. Half were prayed for and the other half were not. The half who were prayed for experienced far less complications, needed far less medication, and recovered much faster.

The basic problem most people have when they pray is they too frequently expect only a positive answer. Many times when God says "no," the "no" turns out to be the best answer for us. I vividly remember two occasions when I prayed long and hard for two specific things. Within a year I learned that, had God said "yes" to the first request, it would have been a disaster for me. It took five years, but I later understood that had He said "yes" to the second request, it too, would have been a disaster. That's the reason we should always pray that God's will be done. He has a bigger, more comprehensive overview of what's going on everywhere.

You Know You're at the Top When ...

9.

You clearly
understand that
failure is an event,
not a person;
that yesterday ended
last night, and today
is your brand-new day.

*Great is his faithfulness;
his lovingkindness begins
afresh each day.*

Lamentations 3:23 TLB

The year was 1888 and the City College of New York was playing a baseball game against Manhattan College. The leading hitter of the CCNY team was a student named "Home Run Lefty." Late in the game, "Home Run Lefty" came to bat with the bases loaded. He hit the ball high over the center fielder's head, allowing the runners before him to score. "Home Run Lefty" was also racing around the bases, desperately trying to beat the throw. The pitcher was covering home plate and caught the throw just as "Home Run Lefty" slid in, knocking the ball from the pitcher's hand.

An argument broke out between the teams. During the free-for-all, "Home Run Lefty" was struck over the head with a baseball bat. Unfortunately, the blow damaged his hearing permanently.

"Lefty's" ambition had been to attend the U.S. Military Academy. However, when his hearing loss forced him to give up his dream, he turned his energies to business. By age thirty he had amassed a fortune and went on to become one of the richest men in the world.

"Home Run Lefty" was undoubtedly disappointed, but he didn't let that stop him. Remember: It's what you do after things happen to you that will make the difference in your career.

You Know You're at the Top When ...

10.

You know that
"he who would be
the greatest among
you must become
the servant of all."

*Whoever desires to become
great among you shall be
your servant.*

Mark 10:43 NKJV

If you're a golf fan, you will remember that John Daly won the British Open in 1995. What you might not know is that there were some "unsung heroes" involved—Corey Pavin, Brad Faxon, Bob Estes, Mark Brooks, and the caddy. The first four were tour players who had also been in the tournament but did not make the playoff.

These four people, along with the caddy, encouraged John and assured him they believed he was going to win, and the caddy was there to help him read those tricky British greens. Put all of that together, along with the fact that Daly was playing unusually well that day, and you have the reason Daly won the British Open. It's true that Daly got all the publicity and all the money, but the question is, "Had those people not been behind the scenes, would he have won the British Open?" The encouragement of others does make a tremendous difference in what we are able to do.

John Daly felt good about winning, and Corey Pavin, Brad Faxon, Mark Brooks, Bob Estes and the caddy also felt good.

The measure of a man is not the number of servants he has but the number of people he serves.

You Know You're at the Top When ...

11.

You are pleasant
to the grouch,
courteous to the rude,
and generous to the
needy because you
know the long-term
benefits of receiving.

Defend the poor and
fatherless; do justice to
the afflicted and needy.

Psalm 82:3 NKJV

Roberta Rich tells a fascinating story about the neighborhood "meanie," a grey-haired man living alone in a weather-beaten corner house.

Timmy badly wanted a bicycle, but there was no money to get one. To earn money, he started going house to house, collecting old newspapers to sell. However, Timmy didn't stop at "Old Meanie's."

One day as Timmy was pulling his wagon through the alley, he saw piles of newspapers stacked almost to the ceiling in the old man's garage. *Wow!* he thought, *I wonder why he just leaves them there?*

The next day Timmy got up enough courage to ring the man's doorbell. To Timmy's surprise, "Old Meanie" invited him in and asked him why he was interested in the newspapers. Timmy explained his purpose, and the old man grinned and said, "A bike, huh? Well, those are bike papers. However, I've got arthritis in my knees now and it's so bad I can't ride one, so I'll just give those papers to you."

Don't be judgmental. Maybe the "Old Meanies" of life have a soft spot that needs touching with a little kindness and attention. Give them what they need (kindness and attention) and you will be ahead of the game—and so will the "Old Meanies."

You Know You're at the Top When …

12.

You recognize,
confess, develop, and
use your God-given
physical, mental,
and spiritual abilities
to the glory of God
and for the benefit
of mankind.

*God has given each of us
the ability to do certain
things well.*

Romans 12:6 TLB

218

Most people in America, almost regardless of their age, recognize the names of Nat "King" Cole and Will Rogers.

Nat "King" Cole started his career as a piano player—not a singer. One night in San Francisco the singer in their ensemble came down with a sore throat. The small club owner proclaimed that if there was no singer, there would be no paycheck. That night Nat "King" Cole became a singer.

Will Rogers was a genuine cowboy and became famous as a trick rope artist. The first five years of his nightclub appearances, he just performed his rope tricks. Then one night someone shouted a question to him and his response brought a burst of laughter. Will Rogers, the humorist, was on his way.

Chances are good that you can neither carry a tune nor do rope tricks, but just as these two men had undeveloped talents inside of them, I'm convinced you, too, have unseen, untapped, unused abilities. Message: Don't sell yourself short. Remember that man was designed for accomplishment, engineered for success, and endowed with the seeds of greatness. That rope trick or song is inside of you. No, perhaps you can't carry a tune, but you do have a song to sing.

You Know You're at the Top When …

13.

You stand in front of the Creator of the universe, and He says to you, "Well done, thou good and faithful servant."

"Well done, good and faithful servant! You have been faithful with a few things; I will put you in charge of many things. Come and share your master's happiness!"

Matthew 25:21

Success, fame, and recognition came to Harvey Pennick at the very end of his life. When he began his career back in the 1920s, Pennick bought a red spiral notebook and started jotting down his observations about the game of golf and the people who play it. In 1991 he finally shared the notebook with a local writer and asked if he thought it was worth publishing. The writer, in turn, showed it to Simon & Schuster and left word with Pennick's wife that the publisher had agreed to print the book for an advance of $90,000.

The next day when the writer saw Pennick, the golfer seemed troubled and finally explained that, with all his medical bills, there was no way he could advance Simon & Schuster $90,000. This genuinely modest man obviously thought Simon and Schuster was asking him for $90,000, instead of offering the money to him.

It's really wonderful to see someone of his incredible ability recognized late in life, while he maintained his modesty to the extent that he could not believe a publisher would pay him that kind of money as an advance. The book sold over a million copies. Through it all, Harvey Pennick, the great teacher, remained modest. That's a marvelous trait for all of us to develop.

About the Author

Zig Ziglar, one of the most popular communicators of his day, is known as the "Motivators' Motivator." More than three million people have attended Zig's live presentations, and millions of others have been inspired by his training tapes and videos. A prolific author, Zig's books have sold more than four million copies worldwide, and his syndicated column, "Zig Ziglar's Encouraging Word," now appears in newspapers nationwide. His long list of awards includes "Communicator of the Year" by the Sales and Marketing Executives International. But what makes Zig most proud, is being happily married to his wife of fifty plus years, Jean, whom he lovingly calls "Sugar Baby."

To obtain additional information on seminars, to schedule speaking engagements, or to write the author, please address your correspondence to:

Zig Ziglar

3330 Earhart, Suite 204

Carrollton, TX 75006-5026

Additional copies of this book and other titles by Zig Ziglar, are available from your local bookstore.

Zig Ziglar's Little Instruction Book
Breaking Through to the Next Level

Honor Books
Tulsa, Oklahoma